From India to Britain to USA and
Canada: An immigrant's story

STRAIGHT FROM
THE HEART

Biography of **Dr Harvinder Sahota**
Famous Cardiologist

Sayantan Chakravarty

Publisher: Sayantan Chakravarty
India Empire Publications

Copyright © India Empire Publications

First Print: July 2017

Design: Jaydev Singh Bisht

Printing Solutions:

India Empire Publications
N 126, 2nd Floor,
Greater Kailash Part 1,
New Delhi - 110048, India.
Tel: +91-11-29231515, 29233647
Mob: +91-9899117477
E: Sayantanc@gmail.com
W: www.indiaempire.com

ISBN No. 978-81-923819-7-8

Cover Photo: Dr Harvinder Sahota (centre). Clockwise from top left: Dr Sahota with Prime Minister Mr Narendra Modi, former PMs Dr Manmohan Singh, Mr I.K. Gujral and Mr Lal Bahadur Shastri, US Ambassador to UN Nikki Haley, former President of Georgia Mikheil Saakashvili, son Neil Sahota with former California Governor Arnold Schwarzenegger, and Sahota with Charles, Prince of Wales

Contents

FOREWORD

*"No man ever steps in the same river twice, for it's
not the same river and he's not the same man"*
—Heraclitus

Sayantan Chakravarty

Orson Wells, producer, co-screenwriter, director and star of the 1941 mystery drama movie *Citizen Kane*—voted on several occasions as the greatest film of all time—would say, "There's no biography so interesting as the one in which the biographer is present." It would be an understatement to say that Harvinder Sahota, incidentally born in the year *Citizen Kane* was made, has been alive and ever present during the production of this biography that has taken about 10 months in the making. He is in fact at the very heart of it, the everlasting soul of this biography, and indeed its exceptional protagonist. His immigrant story is as compelling and riveting as it can get, the narrative is punctuated with pictures which tell a thousand words of their own.

A cardiologist who grew up in different parts of Punjab since his father was posted at various towns by the Indian Railways that employed him, Sahota dreamt of seeing the world from an early age. *The Tribune* newspaper was a regular feature at the Sahota house and young Harvinder grew up reading it from cover to cover, with particular interest in world affairs. It was that interest that made him leave home after completing his graduation in medicine and seek out the world. He went to England to specialize in cardiology, and seven years later, by which time he had brought home a *soni Punjabi kudi* (Asha Sahota, his wife), set out for the New World. He landed in New York in 1974, and from then on swiftly climbed the steps of success. He shot to fame by inventing the perfusion heart balloon, and conducted the angioplasty procedure—which those days was in its infancy—in many parts of the world, including India, for the first time.

He found his moorings in California, a state where he was reluctant to arrive initially for fear of earthquakes, but one where destiny would find him a permanent settlement. It is in Southern California that he has lived since 1977, and apart from excelling in cardiology has tried his hand in business, only to realize that he was not quite cut out for it. Deeply conscious and abiding by the value system instilled in him by his parents, Sahota set up a Chair for Sikh Studies in the name of his beloved mother Bibi Dhan Kaur Sahota at the School of Social Sciences at the University of California at Irvine for a sum of USD 1.5 million. This was to be one among several other Sikh Semester Studies that he has set up at colleges and universities elsewhere in Southern California.

Sahota demonstrates a keen interest in the history of the world. He is a living encyclopedia in happenings and events going on in different parts of the globe and can be a conversationalist's delight. From politics and business, social issues and geography, his areas of knowledge are vast, and tremendous. Time spent with him can be uplifting because he backs

The Publisher with Dr Sahota at the gates of Irvine Cove in Orange County

up his knowledge with lessons from his life experiences. Inside, he remains deeply spiritual and compassionate.

He also remains a generous philanthropist, and socially very active. His interest in political developments is such that he mixes up with leaders across the spectrum, often helping out during campaigns. It comes as no surprise that his childhood interest in happenings around the globe has led him to become a Trustee on the Board of the World Affairs Council of Orange County, an organization with which he spends considerable time and energy.

As you leaf through the pages, this book will serve you many lessons, not least among them in the words of Soren Kierkegaard, the Danish philosopher of repute, that "Life can only be understood backwards, but it must be lived forwards."

Indeed, during the making of this biography, Sahota has been able to review his own life looking backwards, and has spelt out some of the lessons that he's learnt going forwards. Like Orson Wells says, he remains alive and present in this biography, a tribute to his success and integrity as a human being, and as an extraordinary cardiologist.

Sayantan Chakravarty
Publisher
July 2017

FLEDGING THE NEST, SOARING WESTWARD

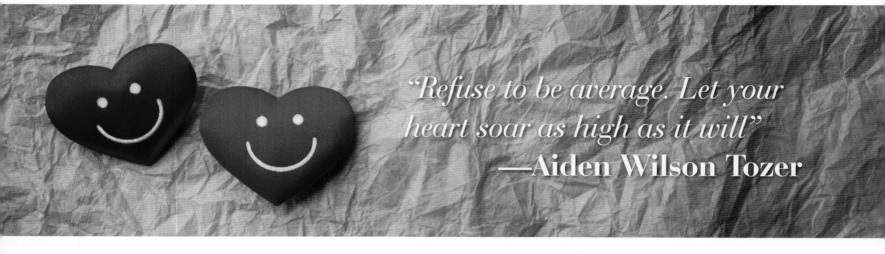

As the Air India aircraft gathered sufficient ground speed at the runway of Delhi's Palam airport and then suddenly lifted its giant frame into the skies, for myriad reasons Harvinder Sahota's heart skipped a beat or two. The young doctor, his face rubbing the window, witnessed the Indian capital city slowly disappearing below the clouds. Also disappearing from view was the country of his birth. Friends and family were now left behind, ahead lay another world yet to be explored. Inside the half-empty aircraft, his pulse raced frenetically. It was the first time in his life that Sahota was flying, that too all by himself and towards a foreign land.

The west was calling. The east was serving him memories.

It is a date—July 15, 1967—that is forever etched in his memory, and emblazoned in his heart. Sahota, now 75, speaks about it in the year 2016 as though things were happening yesterday, so vividly does he recall each moment that day.

Fastened to his seat by a belt he had fiddled with for a considerably long time, his mind had become a blur of emotions and memories. His father, Sardar Lachman Singh, an upright railway official, and his childhood friend Daya Singh had accompanied him in a bus from his native Garhdiwala in Punjab to Delhi. Sahota's mother, Bibi Dhan Kaur, had sewn a new pocket inside his vest. In it he carried the princely sum of Rs 2,300, an amount with which he would later buy a one-way ticket to London from the Air India office at New Delhi's Connaught Place. He would also purchase eight pounds from a money changer in return for 64 rupees, those days the exchange rate for a pound being a mere eight rupees. In contrast, in the autumn of 2016 it stood at 86 rupees, having touched the 100-rupee mark in 2015. At the Palam airport, his father and Daya Singh bid him well. His father blessed him for his onward journey in life. It wasn't going to be an ordinary one by any stretch of imagination, young Sahota's life was about to change, forever.

Inside its pressurized precincts, the aircraft was quiet. Outside, in the center of the clouds, it appeared as if everything was still. The airhostesses and crew made it as comfortable as possible for him, allowing him to settle down and relax. His mind wasn't that still, though. Twenty six years of his existence on earth—specifically in the state of Punjab— had gone by, and now the memories of that significant period in his life whizzed by inside his cranium as he sat close to the window, staring out into the pink and blue horizon. His thoughts took him to the story of his birth into a Sikh family on April 15, 1941 in the Ferozepur Cantonment area. His mother, Bibi Dhan Kaur, whom he greatly reveres, narrated to him how after the midwife had given the one-week old Sahota a bath, he contracted double pneumonia, even though the weather was warm. Now double pneumonia is bad news in 2016, back in 1941 few things could have been worse. In an India still shackled by British rule, the overall health care system was dismal, and infant mortality notoriously high. Antibiotics were not known, perhaps yet to be invented.

Unable to withstand the fury of the inflammatory attack, Sahota's microscopic air sacs inside his baby lungs began to collapse. His inhalation became quite sporadic and he was breathing once every few seconds. Later in life he would come to learn that it was technically called Chain Stoke breathing. In dire situations such as these, family members, relatives, friends and neighbors would usually begin to collect together, knowing that chances of any revival were slim. With hope petering out like sand inside an hourglass, his mother broke down completely. Sahota had turned so cold, and so incorrigibly frigid, that he was declared dead. He was transferred, as per traditions, from his mother's protective arms on to his father's lap. A devastated family was now preparing for the last rites—traditionally, burial, and not cremation, would take place in the case of an infant, or child.

As wail after rising wail rent the air, this is what Sahota remembers of his mother's narration. There existed a door between the Sahota railway quarters and that of their neighbor, much like a vestibule inside a Shatabdi Express. It didn't take long for the lady next door to realize that the infant boy would be taken away for a burial any minute. She stormed inside, shook up her teenage son Hari who was about to enter the washroom, and directed him to rush and get a doctor. Hari who in later years was to become a high official at the Bombay Port did as he was commanded, and bolted out as fast as he could. Several minutes later when the doctor arrived, he saw a large crowd in mourning outside the house, and hesitated from checking on Sahota. "It looks like it's all over," he was overheard saying, "why do I go in?" But Hari insisted that since he'd come all the way, he should take a look at the baby.

When the doctor was about to hold Sahota and confirm what everyone feared, the infant took a breath. His parents could not believe their eyes, and the dark clouds of sorrow started lifting, giving way to the first rays of hope. The doctor knew that the only thing that could save the boy was adequate amounts of oxygen. The Sahota family knew well that there was one oxygen cylinder available at the railway hospital at Ferozepur, and som e family members hurried away to get it. For the second one, Sardar Lachman Singh rushed a friend to Lahore, about half an hour by train. Under British rule, Lahore those days was the capital of undivided Punjab that ran from Peshawar to Delhi, but now lies in the province of Punjab on the Pakistani side. In the early 19th century it was the capital of the Sikh Empire founded by Maharaja Ranjit Singh.

As the first smiles began to break through the lips of his parents, and tears of joy rolled down their faces, his father thanked the doctor profusely for saving his son's life. And at that moment itself Sardar Lachman Singh declared in the presence of all that if indeed this son of his survived the ordeal, he would take all measures to make him a doctor, so that he could go on to alleviate the suffering of others.

Harvinder Sahota had, literally, taken a breath of fresh air that had given him a new lease of life. It happened to be an evening during the month of Ramadan. Praying fervently to God, Bibi Dhan Kaur wanted her son's breathing to become regular. Her prayers were answered, and Sahota's breathing gradually became normal.

Paying respects at the Holy Golden Temple in Amritsar, Punjab, in the mid-1960s

He was named Iqbal at birth. Affectionately, however, they called him Bali, and that was the name with which he was cuddled around the most. Old timers who have known him since his infancy still call him Bali. Others would call him *doctor* during his growing up years, largely because of his father's public proclamation of making him one.

As per tradition, when Sahota was five years old, a religious ceremony was held. Since God had blessed him with a second life, and he had been reborn, the custom was that the priest would open the Sikh holy book—*Guru Granth Sahib*—and pick a stanza whose first letter would be used for renaming. Since in Sahota's case it was the alphabet H, he was given the name Harvinder. In later years when he would graduate from the Patiala Medical College and leave for Britain, his name would be truncated to Harry for the sake of convenience. He recalls that he was playing a badminton doubles tournament at Denbigh in North Wales, when his partner, a Welshman, asked his name. He responded with "Dr Sahota." To which the Welshman said, "No I mean your first name." When Sahota mentioned it was Harvinder, the man offered to cut it short. "Can we make it Harry instead?", he asked.

Ever since, over the last 50 years, for all practical purposes, Harry has become his first name.

He was deeply hooked on to his thoughts on his years in India gone by when the in-flight announcement said that the aircraft was no longer going to stop over at Cairo. War had broken out between the Arabs and Israel, and Air India would give Egypt a miss. Instead, the new layover was going to be in Beirut, Lebanon. Once again Sahota pressed his face against the window to get a view of the Lebanese capital as the aircraft made its descent. But all he saw for a painstakingly long time was plenty of water. At one point he even wondered whether the aircraft would touch down on sea, for he could spot no land. But soon the aircraft touched ground, terminating all such doubts. Beirut airport was a place to explore, and young Sahota decided that he would make the most of his time there. So the next four hours went by fairly quickly as Sahota checked out sundry articles on display at the airport's duty free area, items he had not seen before. He had made one complete flight, and was readying himself for the next one.

London was waiting. So was his tryst with cardiology, and fame. ∎

Perched on a wall in Denbigh Castle in the mountainous countryside of North Wales sometime in 1969

EMPIRE
CALLING

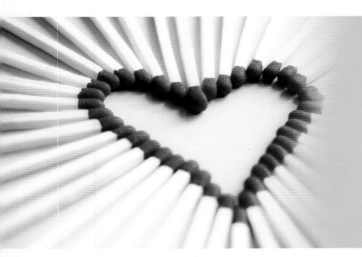

"No one is free who has not obtained the empire of himself"
—**Pythagoras**

For some inexplicable reason the flight from Beirut to London appeared far shorter to Harvinder Sahota than the one from Delhi to the Lebanese capital, even though the distance between the Mediterranean city and the British capital was far longer. One of the reasons could be that while on the flight from Delhi, he had more time to sit back and relax, and even reminisce about the past. This time he was contemplating rapidly on the road ahead. Inside the humming aircraft, Sahota was wondering about the days to come. His mind was seized with thoughts that came naturally to a first-time emigrant.

Had he made the right choice? When he had announced to his father that he planned to go overseas, Sardar Lachman Singh was pleasantly surprised. He told him that he had supported young Harvinder until his education at the Patiala Medical College was over, and he would continue funding him in the future as well. The family had plenty of agricultural land, and orchards, so financial worries would not arise. His son didn't have to go overseas for making more money. Sahota responded to his father in the best and most courteous way possible. He said that he was going overseas not for getting himself a job, not to merely earn more degrees, and least of all for the money. His sole purpose was to see more of the world, something he was keen to do above everything else.

Other questions buzzed through his mind. What was Britain going to be like? What were the likely challenges he was going to face there as a medical practitioner? Would it be a huge change from India in terms of facilities, infrastructure and equipment? Would he be able to overcome the language barrier quickly—after all the colloquial British accent could get difficult to figure?

Would there be psychological hangovers from the days of the Raj, and would he meet with unjustified taunts on the road and in public arenas? Would his British colleagues get along with him easily? Would the women still continue to find him shy? Such questions crisscrossed his mind as he flew over the European continent. But Sahota knew that his answers would come with time, and that was possible only when he started living in England. He was ready to explore, and experience.

Sahota at the Maelor
General Hospital in
Wrexham in August
1972

Sahota in front of his chalet where he lived in Wrexham with Dr Chaudhury (left) from Bihar and Mujeeb Ahmed from Karachi (right) in June 1972

It was somewhere around 6 pm when the Air India flight touched down at London. Thus far, July 15, 1967, had been the longest day in his life. He had gained time flying west, back in India it was 10.30 p.m. The immigration formalities went smoothly. He had to answer a few questions, though. One of them was why he had come to England. Sahota's response was the same as the one he had given his father—he'd come to see the country. He said that he'd stay in England for three years, and then return to India. After all he wasn't fully sure if he had made up his mind to leave India for good.

And soon he was face to face with his cousin Kaka Pritam Singh Sahota, who had been waiting for the young doctor with bated breath, and open arms. The two excited men exchanged greetings, but as soon as they were over, Sahota expressed his first desire on English soil—that of seeing a television set. He had only read about the TV in India, and was curious to now see it for real. Pritam Singh took him over to a shop inside the airport where for the first time Sahota set his eyes on a black and white set. After staring at it intently for a long while, Sahota was ready to leave. Already he became aware that he was in a different world, with people who looked different, and spoke in an unfamiliar accent. Things somehow were quieter and appeared infinitely more orderly than back home. Even as he began to miss some of the chaos back in India, Sahota pinched himself to ascertain that he indeed was on British soil. It was a verification process that did not take very long, and quickly he was back to reality.

Pritam Singh Sahota hailed a cab, and the two cousin brothers were off to London's famous Southall, where they would check into a friend's place for the night. The next day, they were off to Ketley, near Shrewsbury in the Midlands. That is where Pritam Singh lived.

A week later, Sahota decided to visit London and complete some formalities. He entered an instruments store on Gower Street, looking to buy the famous Littman stethoscope. The stethoscope is to the doctor what a sword is to the knight, and a pen is to the bard. Stethoscope around the neck, the doctor's value goes up, and he is set apart from the rest. He chose one particular stethoscope, but the man at the counter asked him for a certain number of "quids" which Sahota couldn't quite comprehend. So he delved into his pocket and flashed out a five pound note, alas it wasn't quite enough to buy that valuable apparatus. He was short by about ten pounds. The counter man noticed his discomfiture, and stepped in to put him at ease. "You can take the stethoscope and send the money later. You need those five pounds more than me," he said. Sahota could not believe what he'd just heard. Here he was, completely unknown to this stranger who did not inquire about his whereabouts, his address, or even his phone number, and was willing to let him walk away with a 15-pound Littman stethoscope. Sahota thanked the man profusely, and first thing next day mailed the money. But till this day it baffles him how a stranger trusted him so much. Was it just a stray act of kindness, or was it the general nature of the British public? Perhaps that was how things were in Britain, and his admiration for the people of England went up.

Fast-forwarding to 1974, he was to have a completely different experience in the USA. He had just landed in Rochester, New York, and was in a store looking for a TV set. When he wanted to pay by check, the salesman asked him for his New York driving license as proof of identity. When Sahota said he

didn't have one, the salesman asked for a credit card. When Sahota replied in the negative again, the salesman asked him why he wasn't paying in cash. Sahota told him he didn't have any cash, and that is why he was offering a check. Suddenly the salesman took Sahota by the arm to a corner and without any warning took the cardiologist's photograph. "Now you can give me your check, and keep your television," he said, quite chuffed with himself that he had not let a customer get away without making a sale.

Sahota recounts that unnerving experience even today. It was vastly different

Sahota was at the North Wales hospital in Llangwyfan (pronounced Kha-leng-wifan), Denbigh between 1969 and 1971. Here he is with senior Nurse In-Charge Mr Jones

from the one in England where he had no check book, and no money, and yet he was allowed to take the Littman stethoscope home. How different America turned out to be. The lack of trust displayed by the TV salesman still rankles him. There are many who have told Sahota that his seven years in England were a waste, he should have headed straight from India to the USA instead. Sahota doesn't quite agree with such people. "I have become what I am because of England. It was the most profitable time of my life" he says. "I learnt not only about medicine, but about life as well. I mean it from the core of my heart." He points out that he'd have been a totally different doctor and human being had he come directly to the USA, and not experienced Britain. His accomplishments in cardiology would have been far lesser too. The stethoscope example in the U.K., and the TV-set experience in the USA, have indelibly imprinted in his heart contrasting feelings about the two countries.

Before he had gone down to Gower Street looking for the Littman stethoscope, Sahota had been to the office of the General Medical Council on 44 Hallam Street. He wished to register himself as a doctor in England, and submitted his documents and certificates, which the GMC found were in order. He was informed that his permanent registration certificate would be mailed to him. On August 18, 1967, the registration certificate arrived. He was now free to practice, and a whole world of opportunities opened up before him. Would he now be able to take up the offer of an opening in Scotland, about which he had learnt from the British General Medical Council, while still in India?

Pritam Singh advised him against moving to Scotland. "It is up north, and considerably colder, and even a touch remote," he told his cousin. While in England he could meet fellow Indians regularly, such a possibility would become rare in Scotland. Sahota, always a prudent decision-maker, gave his cousin's advice some deep thought before abandoning the idea of heading north to Scotland. He was confident that other offers were round the corner. He had read somewhere that if one door was closing, another was opening up somewhere else—so one needn't spend too much time looking at the one that was closing.

His next stop was Bromsgrove Hospital where he was introduced to some consultants by Harmohan Dayal Singh, son of Sahota's teacher at the Patiala Medical College— Professor I.D. Singh. A temporary slot was offered to him as a couple of house officers were going on a month's leave. This turned out to be Sahota's very first job in Britain. One day he was asked to see a male patient that had been suffering from fever for seven days. He diagnosed the man as having Typhoid, and asked the nurses to prescribe him Chloromycetin. The dual words "Typhoid and Chloromycetin" reverberated eerily across the hospital precincts, and created large ripples of anxiety. One of the consultants rushed to Sahota and told him that not only did Typhoid not exist in England, even the medicine he had prescribed was banned. It was a hard lesson he learnt very quickly, and remembers it till this day. When his one-month term got over, Sahota left.

Places like Bromsgrove were to become pit stops in his life. Sahota had set out to see places, and he was not keen to stay put at any one place for too long. That was why he had flown out of India in the first place. He landed up in Wakefield near Leeds and joined the Casualty Department of Clayton Hospital. Mostly emergency cases were brought in here. On his first day he prescribed a rabies injection for a patient that had been bitten by a canine. This time a nurse took him aside and informed him that there was no rabies in England. No typhoid, no rabies—Sahota was indeed learning things! He spent most of his time at Clayton fixing fractures and removing foreign bodies that had

In 1968 at Clayton Hospital, Wakefield (L-R) Mr Dey, Dr Ramnani, Dr Sahota, Dr Singh

surreptitiously made their way into the eyes and noses of people, and were causing them considerable discomfort.

One day a five-year-old girl who had accidentally consumed an entire bottle of hard liquor was rushed to Clayton in a serious condition. Her stomach had to be flushed out and emptied before the girl's condition could be restored back to normalcy. This curious case didn't go unnoticed by the prying media, and local newspapers had a field day reporting the incident. Sahota's stint in Clayton was set to be cut short when his previous employer,

Bromsgrove Hospital, sent him a letter offering him a house job in medicine. Sahota was always keen on medicine, and was not really interested in continuing at the casualty department. He took the letter to the Clayton administration and told them that he would continue with the hospital if they could confirm to him immediately that he would get the same position there. Not entirely to the confident young doctor's surprise the administrator rang up a few consultant doctors and within minutes they offered Sahota a house job in medicine. The job would be his for the next one year. It was a prestigious position for which the hospital would usually advertise, and follow up with interviews. But nothing of that sort happened. Sahota was dictating to the hospital what kind of job he'd like to do. The offer from Bromsgrove was, therefore, not taken up.

A year later, in August 1969, residency term over, Sahota was once again free to choose the course of his career. He drove to Ketley to spend time with his cousin. This time the drive was in his own car, a 10-year-old Hillman Minx, a new acquisition for a mere twenty nine pounds. The car number is etched in his memory—KCP 357. Interestingly, he'd purchased that car from Dr Willis whom he had replaced for the house job in medicine at Clayton, Wakefield. On a lighter note Willis reminded Sahota that he'd taken his job, and even "taken" his car. He had a one year old daughter, now would he want her as well?

In September 1968, he joined the Llangwyfan Hospital in Denbigh in North Wales as a registrar. During his four-year stay at North Wales he was able to take two sabbaticals, the first for a six-month post-graduation course in tropical medicine in 1970 at the Liverpool School of Tropical Medicine. Then in 1971 he went to the University of Cardiff to do a post-graduation in chest medicine, the course once again lasting six months.

Sahota remembers fondly the time he went for an interview for a residency (doctor's house job) from Wakefield to Llangwyfan and sat before an interview panel. There were 15 others apart from him who were waiting to grab that opportunity because a residency in North Wales was a big thing in a doctor's bio. When they asked him about his plans, his answer was the same that he had given his father. He told his interviewers that he'd not come to Llangwyfan to study, or to do a post-graduation. He was merely there because he was interested in taking a look at the country, before returning. Sahota cannot put an exact finger on it, but he guesses that the reason he got the residency over the other waiting candidates was because of his candid response. He didn't try to bluff, and give reasons which weren't true. Admittedly, the interviewers were slightly confounded by his forthrightness about not wanting to study, but they also appeared impressed by his sincerity and honesty. Sahota himself was convinced that his overseas sojourn was to see the world, nothing else. He remains convinced about it up until this day.

Even though he was getting well entrenched in the world of medicine, the life of a bachelor was beginning to unsettle him. Somewhere the loneliness of his existence started gnawing Sahota at the back of his mind. He was missing his family, and the thought of finding a life partner began to earnestly cross his mind. From his younger days, his decisions were always well thought out. This time before picking up his pen, he gave his future a good thought. Then he wrote to his father that he was ready to tie the knot.

When he received his son's missive, Sardar Lachman Singh had to rub his eyes again and again. The entire family had given up on Harvinder Sahota's marriage, he had delayed it way beyond what the customary age back in Punjab was. His siblings were married and settled. Still, when Sahota's two-line message reached his father, he was joyous beyond words. There would be one more celebration in the Sahota family, and it would be a big one.

A new chapter was about to unfold in Dr Harvinder Sahota's life. The Littman stethoscope was no longer going to be his constant companion. He was now readying himself mentally to acknowledge that he would be spending the rest of his time with a life partner. Once again he pinched himself to do a reality check. The girl-shy lad was about to settle down and bid his bachelorhood a final goodbye. ∎

THE TRIBUNE EFFECT

> *"Some billionaires like cars, yachts and private jets. Others like newspapers"*
>
> —Andrew Ross Sorkin

Sardar Lachman Singh's family had somehow weathered the initial storm of Harvinder Sahota's fragile health conditions, and every effort was made to ensure that he grew up into a healthy lad. Time had healed the psychological wounds his family had suffered when he had been declared dead. Things got better with the passage of time, and under the constant protective care and vigil of his mother, Sahota blossomed into a fine boy. Right from a young age it became evident to his family that Harvinder Sahota was cut out for something special.

He was not going to lead an ordinary life. No way was he going to allow himself to be swept away into the sea of mediocrity. The canvas on which he would paint the vision of his future was going to be very large. School was a place where young Sahota found his moorings of early life quickly. His quest for knowledge beyond the immediate limitations of his curriculum, his desire to push himself into a position of respect, kept his adrenalin going. He also realized that a life of too much risk taking was not quite worth it. He would grow up to do something that offered stability, the road to his future would be paved in security,

and not pebbled with uncertainty.

The Sahota family moved frequently due to Sardar Lachman Singh's railway postings, and, therefore, young Harvinder got to study at various schools across Punjab, in Ferozepur Cantonment—where he was born, Garhdiwala, Jalandhar and Pathankot. His inquisitive and sharp mind enjoyed every minute of his growing up. The postings of his father helped Sahota gain valuable insight into the life of ordinary Punjabis, and how things were shaping up for them in a young, independent India in the late 1940s and 1950s. The British were gone, but so had most of the opportunities.

Due to the frequent change of towns, Sahota would make friends, only to have to let them go when his father moved. But early in his teens he developed a constant companion in *The Tribune,* a newspaper he credits for giving him a rounded world view, and for building inside him a deep urge to explore Britain, Europe and America. It was through the pages of this newspaper, always delivered early morning at the Sahota home no matter which town or city they lived, that he came to know of

political and social developments in different continents, and read with more than a great deal of interest about what world leaders were saying. His astute mind learnt to read between the lines quite early, and tried to discern each time whether these men meant what they said, or said what they meant. He understood the manipulations of politics, and the undercurrents of deception. Even now, as he sits inside his tastefully-decorated mansion at Irvine Cove in the city of Laguna Beach, Sahota cannot help but flip through a series of news channels in order to get a more balanced world view. He describes himself as a complete "news junkie", which he truly is, and can talk on almost any subject with a great deal of vigor and energy. He tops up his diet of printed news with a generous dose of history that he comes across on some select channels.

Classmates and friends in Patiala Medical College in the 1960s. (L-R) Harbhajan Singh Girgla of Delhi, Sahota, Kundan Singh Lidhar from Jalandhar, Baldev Raj Bhandari from Gurdaspur, Daya Singh Arora from Amritsar

(Above) The group of five stayed close together during college days

(Facing Page) A trip from the Patiala Medical College to Agra in February 1961. Professor Thind is in the center, while a shy Sahota is behind the ladies

It was the year 1957 that he passed out of the M.B. Higher Secondary School in Pathankot, completing his matriculation with aplomb. But there was a twist, he was now thinking of changing the course of his career. He had been an incorrigible film buff, and had watched most of the Hindi movies that would hit Punjab theaters those days. The black and white movies with their dream merchant heroes and beautiful actresses had sown the seeds of acting in Sahota's mind. The same year he and childhood friend Daya Singh decided that they'd leave for Bombay, as Mumbai was known then. That is where the film industry flourished, and Sahota would try out his skills as an actor. The two were to meet at the railway station, but Daya Singh failed to show up at the last minute. Later, Sahota came to know that his friend had received a job offer from the Life Insurance Corporation of India, and his family much preferred that Daya Singh settle down, instead of foraying into something as uncertain as a life in the film world. Not without pain, Sahota saw the train to Bombay leave before his eyes. With abundant reluctance he dropped his plans of proceeding alone, shelving his dreams of becoming a part of the rough and tumble of the film industry, and decided that the best option was to dig his heels deep into the world of medicine.

The Bombay dream was over, but the Jalandhar story was just unfolding.

Soon he joined the FSc Medical DAV College in Jalandhar for his pre-university degree, thus taking the first step on way to becoming a doctor.

GETTING PAST RESERVATION

It wasn't going to be a walk in the park though. Getting into medical college was going to be tough. Punjab had two medical colleges, one at Patiala and the other at Amritsar. The one at Patiala had only 80 seats

for medical students, and thousands were competing to get in. Twenty per cent of those seats were reserved for girls, thus giving a new twist to the stiff competition. Another five per cent were reserved for those from economically weaker sections. But still Sahota made it to the Patiala Medical College easily, and got admitted in 1959. It was a proud moment for the Sahota family, especially his father, whose dream he had fulfilled. For the very first time in his life he was in a co-educational institution. It was a real challenge, for he'd never studied alongside girls before!

Unusually laconic, and typically studious, Sahota did not even make feeble attempts to impress his fellow students, especially those of the opposite sex, neither with any kind of swagger, nor with typical smart-Alec quips. Unlike some of his college mates who may have been given to bluster and some long-winding torrents of verbosity from time to time, Sahota kept his comments to himself, and did not bother to mix around much, mostly keeping himself confined to his hostel room where he had his curriculum books to contend with. Perhaps this quality of being reserved made him an all-

Sahota with the coveted MBBS degree

हे राम

round attraction. In the first week itself he was unanimously elected secretary of the Patiala Medical College. It came as a surprise, when fellow student Harbans Singh came up to him and said, "We have unanimously decided that you should be the secretary of our Medical College, and no one will contest against you." There was one student, though, who was not agreeable to this idea and wanted to pit himself against Sahota, but pressure from fellow students soon made him drop the idea.

Sahota did not have to canvas at all to get the position of secretary. And significantly he was saved the bother of having to campaign outside the girls' hostel, a thought he actually dreaded. He was indeed very shy, and could hardly speak up when seated next to a girl, or even look her in the eye. Fellow girl students, in a lighter vein, never refrained from pointing out his lack of garrulity, but secretly they may have admired him for it.

Sahota was a natural leader. When he was

Sahota at Delhi's Raj Ghat with childhood friend Daya Singh (second from right) where Lal Bahadur Shastri had come immediately after being sworn in as Prime Minister of India on June 9, 1964. Shastri was paying homage to Mahatma Gandhi at his *Mahasamadhi*

in junior high in Jalandhar and had just moved from the fourth to the fifth grade, he realized this aspect in his character. He was seated in his new class somewhere in the middle rows when on the very first day the teacher in-charge came in to the class, pointed at him, and announced that Sahota would be class monitor. He then asked Sahota, the "boy in the bush shirt", to come over and stand next to him. This way the teacher let the class know in no uncertain terms who would be their leader from then on.

Sahota, of course, links his childhood reticence in the presence of girls to his own upbringing and growing up with five sisters, and his mother's value-system which she had passed diligently on to her son. "I did not feel the need to respond, just for the sake of saying something," he clarifies, several years down the road.

As medicine slowly grew on him, so did the world. *The Tribune* kept flashing across news items every day, and he inevitably found the time away from his thick medical books to devour them. The ones that interested him the most were happenings around the world. It is a trait that has not deserted him till date. You can see him watching world news with the interest of a man readying himself to run for President.

But president he had once become. Sahota's charismatic character ensured victory for him in a three-way contest for college president while he was in his second year. The number of votes he received was substantially higher than other contestants. Even women readily voted for the taciturn Sahota, but the congenital coyness refused to ebb. Then one day, mustering enough courage, he decided that his class—comprising both boys and girls—ought to see the Taj Mahal—one of the seven wonders of the world— and hired a bus for that purpose. A fellow student spoke to someone at the Prime Minister's office, and Mr Nehru, India's PM, agreed to meet the students at his official residence in New Delhi—at that time it was in the Teen Murti House.

But the meeting wasn't to be. The bus driver was hastily making his way through a railway crossing and banged the vehicle hard against a pillar. Immediately, the vehicle carrying the students broke down, and hopes of meeting Prime Minister Nehru evanesced into thin air. Sahota does recall, though, that Mr Nehru mentioned about the damaged bus incident at a speech that he gave later that day. On another occasion, the class made a trip to Chandigarh, the capital city of Punjab. The high point was boating at the lake, which lingers on vividly in Sahota's memory from the early 1960s.

He wasn't to meet Nehru, but Sahota and Daya Singh were at Rajghat—Mahatma Gandhi's *Mahasamadhi*—when Lal Bahadur Shastri came there to pay homage to the great soul, right after he'd been sworn in as Indian Prime Minister on June 9, 1964. Shastri was succeeding Nehru as PM. Sahota recalls that there was no entourage and no accompanying security. There was no media presence, and he could hardly see any cameraman around. There were five or six persons with Shastri. He overheard some people say that Indira Gandhi, Nehru's daughter, had eventually relented and had agreed to take up a ministerial position in Shastri's Cabinet—she would later receive the important Information and Broadcasting portfolio. Until then, Indira had been mourning the passing away of her father, and had declined offers to join the Government. Nehru had died just two weeks earlier, on May 27, 1964.

While at the Patiala Medical College, young Sahota made up his mind that he would leave India when the opportunity presented itself. It wasn't going to be about the money, it was going to be all about getting to know newer places, and discovering more of the planet. Patiala would be the stepping stone to his onward journey into the world.

By 1967, the opportunity had presented itself.   ∎

WEDDING BELLS

"There's a higher form of happiness in commitment"
—Claire Forlani

It was while at Cardiff that Sahota felt like he needed to make a commitment to a life partner. Even though he was enjoying the life of a medical doctor, somewhere a tinge of loneliness at being far away from home must have begun to set in. He was past 30, and the idea of marriage had started germinating in his mind. The shy young man who wouldn't look girls in the eye at college was now contemplating spending the rest of his life with a woman.

He remembers vividly the moment when he made up his mind about marrying. He was driving down to the hospital at Llangwyfan from Cardiff. Llangwyfan was like a pit-stop for European medical students in England while they looked for other opportunities. And Cardiff was where he'd just completed his post-graduation. He was on the wheel of a brand new Austin Mini 1000 – OUN 113G when Sahota made his decision. He reached his workplace and wrote to his father about his new desire.

It was June 1971, and the Sahota family was pleased as Punch. They immediately set out to look for a *sohni kudi* for their *vilayati munda*—a pretty girl for their settled-in-England son. In six months he'd be flying down to India

for the marriage, and things needed to be speeded up.

When he was all set to leave for India on December 16, 1971, little did Sahota know that there would be a twist in his tale, a sting in the tail of his marriage plans. As he waited for his cousins to pick him up and drop him at Heathrow, Sahota switched on the TV. The news flash that he saw sent alarm bells ringing in his mind. War had broken out between India and Pakistan. East Pakistan wanted to be liberated from the clutches of West Pakistan, and India was helping it in its cause.

Sahota spoke to his travel agency, but was informed that his flight to New Delhi was on. As they closed in towards Birmingham, there was another news flash, this time on the car radio. The words of the news reader were clear and sharp—all flights to the Indian capital had been cancelled. The gravity of the situation began to sink in. His marriage plans were shelved for now, war had come as an absolute damper. Flustered at having to return back, Sahota decided to cancel his leave, and immerse himself in his work at his North Wales hospital in Llangwyfan.

It wasn't until February 1972 that he was able to leave

for India, this time via Moscow on an Aeroflot plane. Once he reached Garhdiwala, he ran into emotional parents, siblings and friends. The bride-hunting had been on in full flow, and it seemed that the exigencies of war had failed to dampen the enthusiasm of those who were doing the match-making. Girl after girl was introduced to the *vilayati munda,* but he didn't seem all too impressed, until, of course, he met Asha. She was a young captain in the Indian army and also a medical doctor posted in Delhi. She's born in Punjab but had grown up in Ranchi. She had attended the Bishop Westcott Girls High School there. Subsequently she had graduated from the Patna Medical College about 800 miles east of Patiala Medical College, Sahota's own alma mater. At the time Asha was a student, Ranchi and Patna were part of Bihar, with the latter being the

Wedding cake being cut at the reception held inside the compound of the hospital in Wrexham

Asha Sahota making *chapatis* in the chalet kitchen at Wrexham sometime in March 1973. Harvinder and Asha had married in England in December 1972

state capital. While Patna continues to remain the capital of Bihar, Ranchi is the capital of Jharkhand, a new state. Asha's father Niranjan Singh Claire worked with Bird and Co in Bihar. It was a private British firm headquartered in Calcutta that was to be taken over by the Indian Federal Government in 1974, and was also one where Indian cinema's superstar Amitabh Bachchan had worked before deciding to

enter the film world in Bombay. Claire was a mining engineer at the time with the company. He and Asha met with Sahota at the officers' mess in Delhi, but the reason behind the meeting remained mostly unknown to Asha until after the doctor from North Wales had bid goodbye for the evening.

As Claire Forlani says, there's a higher form of happiness in commitment. Sahota knew almost immediately after the meeting that committing himself to marry Asha would make him happy. He informed her father accordingly. Niranjan Singh said he'd seek his daughter's opinion before finally giving the final approval. Asha's "yes" took a little while coming, but eventually it did. It seems she may not have been too keen to leave India, but something told her that the choice she was making about her marriage was the best one. Soon the two were engaged. In April, Sahota decided it was time to return. This time, though, when Sahota was leaving for England, there were four people to see him off at Delhi airport. Along with Niranjan Singh, there were two of Sahota's brothers. And there was Asha. For the first time Harvinder Sahota and Asha exchanged a few words. When Harvinder asked her what she'd like from England, she wrote down the name of a couple of books in his diary along with her address. Once he was back at the Maelor General Hospital in Wrexham in North Wales, Harvinder started writing regularly to his would-be-bride. He inevitably received prompt responses.

There's a fairly long and formal process of leaving the Indian Armed forces, especially for a commissioned officer. Asha could expedite that process on the grounds of her impending marriage. But several documents were required, among them certified ones from British magistrates seeking her discharge. Letters followed to the British High Commission in Delhi for her visa. Then a period of wait ensued, as the Government of India needed to clear her application. On the other side of the world, Sahota who had the gift of making things happen, had managed to arrange for Asha's residency in obstetrics and gynecology at the Maelor General Hospital.

A decision was made that Sahota would marry Asha in England. And so, exactly a year after Sahota had been forced to postpone his wedding plans, Asha landed up in London.

It was December of 1972, and things were very cold in England. After meeting her groom-to-be at Heathrow, Asha left for Leicester with an uncle. The civil marriage was set for a weekend, Saturday, December 16, 1972.

But when the appointed hour came, there happened to be another little twist in the story. This time Asha's uncle who had been in a tearing hurry to reach the marriage registrar's office had forgotten a minor detail—to pick up his niece, Asha, and bring her to the venue. By the time Asha arrived, several other marriages had been put on hold. Asha, looking resplendent in a red saree, and Sahota received healthy coverage in the local media for the wedding. The reception was held at the compound of Wrexham hospital, a place where Sahota recalls champagne flowed generously. Perhaps the only man who was not drinking was Sahota himself, as he was a teetotaler. The couple's relatives and friends turned up in good numbers to celebrate. After dinner at Chester in the evening, the couple moved in to Sahota's staff quarters at the hospital. By Monday, Asha had begun her residency.

Sahota sees Asha's residency as an exceptional event in his life. It wasn't easy finding a residency job in England and here was Maelor General Hospital creating space for his would-be-wife who was still in India. She got the job without the hospital advertising for one, without herself having to appear for an interview, and while still in India. It was a rare feat! That is how much the hospital had wanted to retain Sahota after he put conditions that his bride should also find work at the same place. "Indeed they went out of their way to create a job for Asha," Sahota reminisces.

About a week after their marriage they ran into a couple who instantly recognized the Indian pair. Their own wedding had been delayed because Asha's uncle had forgotten to pick her up. It led to some humorous leg-pulling, of course. ∎

SETTLING DOWN
IN CALIFORNIA

> *"Southern California, where the American Dream came too true"*
> —**Lawrence Ferlinghetti**

When a man can keep a commitment, he invariably raises himself in the eyes of others. Martin Luther King was committed to non-violence. Henry Luce, the founder of *Time* magazine, demonstrated commitment by raising the standards of journalism at the world level. George Washington was committed to the idea of America and eventually took it to an inspiring conclusion. Sam Walton of Walmart knew that if he committed himself to being the best that he could be, the rest of the things would fall in place—in fact, they invariably did.

In his own way, Harvinder Sahota always knew the importance of commitment, and he didn't let himself down. He fulfilled his commitment of spending about a year in Regina in Saskatchewan, Canada, a sparsely populated place where temperatures plummet to -50 F in winters. He need not have gone to Regina. After all Rochester Hospital in New York was offering him a hundred thousand dollars a year plus benefits back in 1976. It was an astronomical sum of money at that time, and yet he walked away from it because he'd already informed the administration in Regina that he would be joining them after his fellowship in New York was done. The commitment to Regina had been made while he was in England.

At the end of his 11-month term in the hospital in Regina, the snowy and cold capital of Saskatchewan Province in Canada, Sahota knew that he would be looking for greener pastures, literally. Regina, the second-largest city in the province after Saskatoon, is a cultural and commercial center for southern Saskatchewan. Wascana used to be the seat of the Government of remote North-West Territories which included, before bifurcation, the current provinces of Saskatchewan and Alberta. In 1882, Wascana was renamed Regina, which in Latin means Queen, by a decision made by Princess Louise, who was the Duchess of Argyll, and the wife of the Governor General of Canada—in honor of her mother, Queen Victoria. There is also a statue of Queen Elizabeth II on horseback in front of the Saskatchewan Legislative Building in Regina.

Dr Gerald Ewing, Sahota's good friend, was Director

Sahota in August 2016 stands in the shade just outside the first house he ever owned—one at the City of Seal Beach where he and his family spent 19 years between 1978 and 1997

of Programmes at Regina, while Sahota himself was Chief Medicine Resident. Dr Ewing asked him about his future plans, and Sahota said he was yet to decide. Meanwhile, the University of Saskatchewan showed a great deal of earnest intent in not letting Sahota go away by offering him a position in cardiology, and even depositing a month's salary into his bank account. Sahota had valid immigration documents, and if he had wished, he could have stayed back in Regina. But the 36-year-old cardiologist politely returned the salary, saying he needed to explore other

Sahota breaks into a smile seeing the lovely yellow-lemon tree in full blossom at the Seal Beach house

opportunities, this time in the USA. Dr Ewing himself called up some doctor friends in Los Angeles and asked if they required somebody talented to join them. When the answer was in the affirmative, it meant it was time for Sahota and his family to bid goodbye to Regina and head to California. Sahota was to join the St Vincent Medical Center in Los Angeles from July 1, 1977 on a fellowship that would be his third, after the ones at Rochester in New York, and Regina in Saskatchewan.

Sometime in June 1977, with Sahota at the wheel of his Datsun B-210 and Asha and Neil alongside, began the family's ten-day, 1,700-mile drive to Los Angeles. They would eventually cut across the states of Montana, Idaho, Utah, Nevada before entering California. It was the same sturdy machine in which they had driven from Rochester to Regina. The Sahotas would break journey several times, including at Las Vegas, where for the first time they witnessed in awe a kaleidoscope of glittering lights, casinos and slot machines. When little Neil tried to go near one of the machines, a security man gently handed him over to his parents since children weren't allowed. Three-year-old Neil, in his innocence, had tried pushing the buttons. The weather in Las Vegas in June was extremely hot, a sudden change from the cooler climes of Regina, and the family wasted little time in getting into the showers. After spending a day at the glamour city, the Sahotas arrived in Los Angeles. The date was June 30, 1977.

The family tried checking in at a hotel nearby but it turned out to be unsuccessful because they did not want a child. After a while the staff relented, and the Sahotas stayed a night there. Shortly, they found accommodation at another hotel called the Nuttel-Muttel, not too far from SVMC. Sahota started work at the Medical Center on July 1, 1977. It's a date that he can never forget, for his California adventure was just beginning.

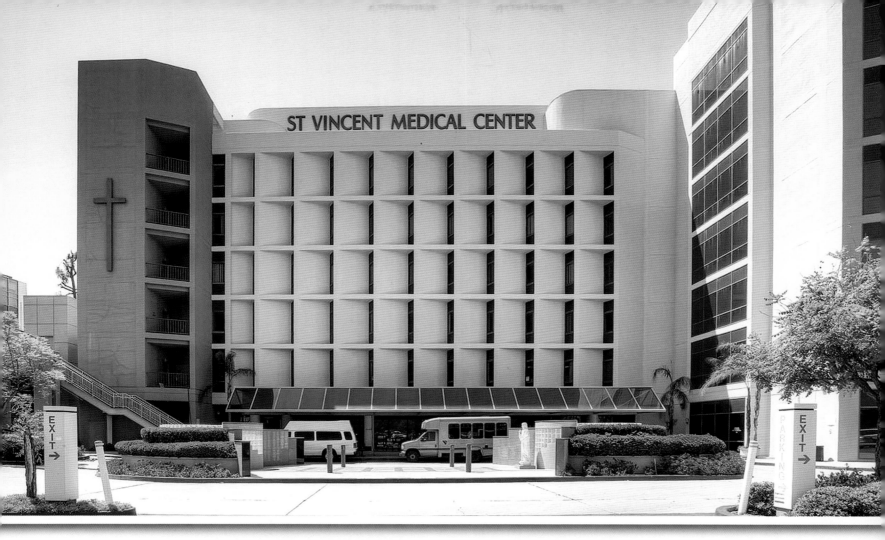

A present day picture of St Vincent Medical Center in Los Angeles.
Sahota had joined this place on July 1, 1977 on a Cardiology Fellowship

Soon they were looking for an apartment to stay. Finding one turned out to be an arduous affair, most owners did not want children. Fortunately, when they were at the local Sikh Gurudwara, they ran into a man who turned out to be an alumnus of the Patiala Medical College, several years Sahota's junior. He offered to show them a place at Pasadena, about 10 miles away. Here they got hold of a local newspaper, and pored over the sections that offered apartments on rent. Finally when they found one that allowed children, the owner let them know that the place was not quite clean. By then a fair bit of desperation had set in, and Asha quickly said that she would clean it herself, and wouldn't wait for help. And that is how their stay at Pasadena began. It happened to be a historic day— America had just completed 201 years of its independence. Soon they were to discover that there was not a single piece of utensil at the place. But all shops were closed on July 4. The owner helped them with some plates, cups, pans and pots, and things were off and running.

Following a test, Sahota got a California car driving

license and gradually became accustomed to the trip between his house in Pasadena and SVMC in Los Angeles in the Datsun, his old buddy. He was doing quite well, earning USD 1,500 a month, a vast improvement over the USD 800 that he was getting in Regina. But still it did not compare with the Rochester offer that he had forgone in order to keep his tryst with Regina. A year later, on June 8, 1978, the Sahotas welcomed into their world their second child, another son. Asha named him Eric which is a Norse word for someone who's an Eternal Ruler. Unlike in Neil's case, the middle name Singh was added, making him Eric Singh Sahota.

On the work front, meanwhile, Sahota had started doing so well that his income doubled within a year. It would help in many ways. When Asha was expecting the couple's second child, Sahota wanted to move to a more comfortable place, and was on the lookout for a house of his own. Just before Eric was born, he narrowed down and bought a place in the City of Seal Beach in Orange County for USD 130,000. By then, in the over three years that he had spent in the USA and Canada, Sahota had saved about USD 10,000, an amount which was utilized for making a down payment for the house. For the rest, he took two loans: one of USD 40,000 from the seller of the house, and another USD 80,000 from the bank. The money that was being paid for rent would now take care of the mortgage.

In August 1978 they moved into their new house. It needed a fair bit of renovation, and Asha thought that the carpets needed immediate replacement. Along with looking after the house, she now had to take care of little Eric, and Neil who was attending kindergarten. Sahota, of course, was soaring professionally, and the decision of Asha not practicing medicine had been a wise one for the family. Things were motoring along quite well, and California was growing on the Sahotas with each passing day. ∎

Sahota narrates an anecdote in one of the bedrooms of the Seal Beach house while standing next to a small, black and white television set from yesteryears

HEADY AND HECTIC TIMES

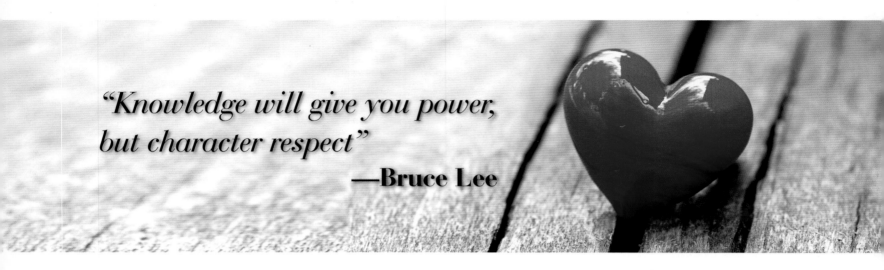

*"Knowledge will give you power,
but character respect"*
—Bruce Lee

ndreas Roland Gruentzig was a Switzerland-based German radiologist who was the pioneer of the balloon angioplasty. He performed the first angioplasty in Zurich on September 16, 1977. Having heard about this epic event which received wide coverage worldwide, Dr Sahota decided that he would fly down to Zurich, meet Gruentzig, and if the possibility presented itself, he'd see a live angioplasty demonstration. But sometime in late 1977, Dr John Sorensen, a cardiologist from Utah who also was on a fellowship at the St Vincent Medical Center (SVMC) in Los Angeles, informed Sahota that Gruentzig was trying to line up a visit to the USA, and, therefore, Sahota need not fly down to Zurich. Sahota had to wait a while, though, because Gruentzig eventually performed the first live angioplasty demonstration in the USA only in 1980.

Professionally, Sahota's life was to change very soon, and become much more fast-paced. By the end of 1981, having learnt hugely from Gruentzig's immensely significant procedures, Sahota was performing angioplasty in the USA. He became known as this dexterous

cardiologist who was carrying out the novel procedure that brought huge relief to his patients. In the next five to seven years his cardiology practice bloomed and took him to great heights. He became a name in the USA, and beyond, and even back in India. All this, of course, meant that his hours of work kept getting stretched. Along with rising fame came a hectic lifestyle, and somehow he allowed himself to be swept into the vortex of it all. He was waking up early to meet the demands on his time. Typically his day would start at 4 a.m. He would hit SVMC early for procedures. If he was not doing angioplasty then he'd be busy helping out surgeons who needed a cardiologist as part of the team that performed heart surgeries.

Later in the day he'd see patients, carry out consultations, handle emergency cases. By the time he'd be back with his family—Asha, Neil and Eric—it would be way too late to have any meaningful conversations. Certainly the boys were missing out on their father due to the breakneck nature of his work. Sahota knew it, and tried desperately to balance his life. When some relatives of the Sahotas who had just moved in to the USA complained

Dr Sahota (standing fourth from left, front row) among cardiologists from all over the world at the Emory University, Atlanta, Georgia in 1980 where Dr Andreas Gruentzig (standing eleventh from left, front row in brown coat), considered the father of angioplasty, gave the first ever demonstration of this pioneering procedure in the USA

about how hard their life had become in the new country, the heart doctor would talk about his own 20-hours-a-day routine, and they'd all fall silent. You could hear a pin drop after that.

Around 1988, he entered into discussions with the Postgraduate Institute of Medical Education and Research (PGIMER) in Chandigarh for carrying out the first ever angioplasty procedure in India. Putting together a team that'd accompany him along with necessary equipment took a while. Finally on January 15, 1990, at the invitation of Professor P.L. Wahi, Director at

PGIMER, and Dr I.S. Anand, Additional Professor of Cardiology at the same institute, Sahota performed the first angioplasty in India. He was overwhelmed with emotion and nostalgia when this news made headlines in *The Tribune*, the newspaper Sahota would read from front to back right from the time he was a teenager in India. It was the same newspaper that had been able to arouse his curiosity about the world, and had shaped his desire to see different places. Even though through the 1980s he had performed several hundred angioplasty procedures, hitting the headlines in *The Tribune* meant a lot. After all,

Young Neil (top) and his younger brother Eric (top right) pose for the cameras many summers ago. During his hectic days as a cardiologist in the 1980s, Sahota would see less and less of them because of his long hours, and transcontinental travels

(Facing page) Harvinder and Asha Sahota on board an Alaska Cruise, *Celebrity Mercury*, on August 8, 2008

he was being recognized back in his ancestral state from where his life journey had begun. He and his team members with whom he visited the Holy Golden Temple at Amritsar were feted and felicitated after their feat. When Sahota explained to the people that angioplasty eliminated the potential risks involved in open-heart surgery and also substantially reduced the financial burden on the patient, the procedure started gaining popularity in India.

It was in October 1990 that he was invited to perform the first angioplasty in Mexico. He went to Guadalajara, a city known as Mexico's cultural capital, and one that had hosted many soccer matches during the FIFA World Cup in 1970 (it would host more during the 1986 FIFA World Cup). Soon after he'd carried out the procedure, he received a handsome offer to move his base from Los Angeles to Guadalajara. But Sahota politely declined the offer, unwilling to ruffle the stable life he was used to in Los Angeles.

More invitations were to follow. In 1991 he travelled to Leningrad (now St Petersburg) in the USSR, a city that is, incidentally, twinned with Guadalajara. But

Inside the Cath Lab at the PGIMER, Chandigarh

Sahota in St Petersburg in May 1991 with a
Russian cardiologist and Dr Jose Farinha (right) from California

the hospitals at Leningrad were not quite ready for him to perform angioplasty. Quite similar was the case in Moscow. Sahota had read in newspapers that there were more female doctors than male ones in Russia. He wanted to find out more and asked a top Soviet heart surgeon about this curious anomaly. He received a surprising answer—Sahota was told that in the Soviet Union those days, the Government's socialistic policies were based on the assumption that human needs were more or less similar. In other words, it was assumed that there was not much difference between the basic needs of a doctor and that of a chauffeur, which also implied that there wasn't much difference in salary levels between the two. The real picture, therefore, was that men did not easily wish to go through the long haul of studying medicine for years, and not getting paid very well after that. Women on the other hand did not mind working harder for less remuneration.

NO WAY JOSE

When he was in Russia, Victory Day was being celebrated. It commemorates the triumph of the Soviet Union over Nazi Germany with the signing of the German Instrument of Surrender on May 9, 1945. He and his colleague Jose Farinha booked themselves at *Hotel Russia* which at the time was the largest hotel in the world, a giant 21-storeyed edifice with 3,000 rooms overlooking the Kremlin at Red Square, a concert hall, a movie theater, a barber shop, a police station, a nightclub, a post office and a health club. In 1990, though, it was to be beaten to second place in terms of size and capacity by the *Excalibur* in Las Vegas, Nevada. Eventually, *Hotel Russia* shut down in 2006. As they slowly walked towards the elevator to check in to their rooms, three Russian girls asked them where they were from. When Sahota replied he was from America, one of them said, "Oh…America, America, do you want to have sex?" He glanced nervously at his colleague, and his response seemed to be something like, "No way Jose…" Farinha, though, wanted a moment to understand if what he was hearing inside the lobby of the world's largest hotel was indeed true. Sahota, meanwhile, dashed for the elevator and disappeared.

It was the second week of May 1991 when he flew to Ukraine where in the capital city of Kiev a patient was lined up for angioplasty. From there he went to Tbilisi, the capital of the Republic of Georgia. Here they were not yet ready for angioplasty, so Sahota had discussions and gave a few lectures. He also met up with old friends and extended his commitment to work with them in future. From there he went to Moscow, but here too, like in Tbilisi, the doctors were not ready to do the angioplasty procedure.

Exactly a year later in May 1992 he returned to Moscow where he performed the first complex coronary angioplasty alongside his friend Dr Nick Kipshidze. Since he was in

great demand in the medical fraternity, Sahota returned to PGIMER several times in the 1990s to deliver lectures on the advances that he had made through his own inventions and methods of angioplasty. In 1995, he met with Dr Purushottam Lal of Metro Hospital in the city of Noida in Uttar Pradesh, bordering Delhi, and carried out several angioplasty procedures there. In fact the demonstrations were broadcast live in the local cable network for the benefit of citizens living in the vicinity.

The team members that flew in from Los Angeles to carry out the first angioplasty procedure in India seen outside the bus that transported them from Delhi to Chandigarh and back. (L-R) Dr M Choi, Dr Sahota, Dr Jose Farinha (all cardiologists), Anna Hall, Denise Gombrich (both nurses), Steve Bellows and Nicole Gordon (Cath Lab technicians). Dr Sahota was leading the team

Dr Sahota with an elite group of heart surgeons and cardiologists at Leningrad, USSR, in May 1991. He was to return in May 1992 to the USSR to do the first angioplasty procedure. Leningrad was later renamed St Petersburg

Although he remained very busy in his own private clinic and in the management of cardiology practices, Sahota would invariably find time to lecture and educate audiences at different places across the world. Those who heard him included medical students, nurses, physician assistants, doctors. He spoke at community gatherings as well. Besides, he spent time on new inventions in cardiology. For doing so much work outside his own practice, indeed a rarity among doctors who practice privately, Sahota's name is being recommended for the Nobel Prize. The recommendations list the number of inventions that he has against his name, introduction of the procedure of angioplasty in several countries across the world, finding time to lecture, teach and research on top of his regular workload, managing a busy cardiology practice where, besides his clinic at Bellflower City, he's been associated with a number of leading hospitals in the Greater Los Angeles area. Combining so many aspects of cardiology is indeed a unique facet in any one single doctor.

Dr Sam Singh of Bakersfield first met Sahota in 1977. He has followed his work closely, and knows how much commitment and dedication he has shown to the profession of cardiology by practicing, inventing, lecturing and more. He says, "I know Dr Sahota from the time we both were doing our fellowships at the St Vincent Medical Center. He is a very good cardiologist, highly honest, straightforward and knowledgeable about world affairs."

Indeed, Sahota is fortunate that his peers admire him for who he is. No doubt those times in the 1980s and 1990s were indeed very heady, and hectic, for him. He always walked that extra yard and kept pushing the envelope when it came to his profession. He has shown the world that he has deep knowledge of his craft, but it is the way that he has handled his fame that has determined his character. No wonder recognition and respect have walked in through his door time and again. ∎

"HARRY LET'S GO TO PUNJAB"

Could Dr Sahota's life have been different? Well, at some point he tried to make it different, but his plans of becoming a businessman came apart. There's no doubting the success he achieved professionally. As Colin Powell who served at the highest levels of American Government observes, there are no secrets to success, one has to prepare and work hard. Sahota had worked very hard all his life, prepared himself exceedingly well, and learnt how to get things right in his profession. But when he did make an attempt at business, things did not work out. It wasn't so much failure on his part, as it was indecisiveness on the part of those on whom he depended. It turned out be another of life's lessons, a learning curve he'd remember for a very long time. He's better off for that.

It was in 1980 that Sahota had been part of a very large angioplasty demonstration in Atlanta with the elite cardiologists of the world in attendance. Enthused by his Georgian experience, Sahota became an angioplasty practitioner, and set very high standards in his field. He became an easily recognizable name in the industry, and his clientele grew steadfastly. He became one of the earliest medical doctors in America to start using the over-the-wire system.

Because of his indisputable skills, high success rate, the name he had earned in his field, and, of course, the Punjab connection, he was invited by the Post Graduate Institute of Medical Education and Research, Chandigarh, to perform the angioplasty procedure. It was sometime in the late 1980s that Sahota, accompanied by a team of cardiologists, nurses, lab technicians, and a planeload of instruments, arrived in Delhi and then drove down to the capital city of Punjab. When he performed the very first angioplasty procedure at the PGIMER, it made headlines in *The Tribune,* the paper Sahota had read so extensively during his days in Punjab. It was an amazing feeling to be recognized in his home state in India, that too after having spent so many years overseas. "The feeling was simply indescribable," says Sahota. Even the *Indian Express*, another large newspaper with pan-India editions, interviewed him at length. It gives him a high even today to recount those memories.

Sahota was honored to host Mikheil Saakashvili at his house in 2011. Saakashvili who was President of Georgia at the time was slotted to stay at Sahota's Laguna Beach house for an hour, but extended it by another two hours. Pleased by the generous hospitality, he asked Sahota if he wanted to open a Punjabi restaurant in Tbilisi, the capital of his country

Soon his good friend and cardiologist, Dr Nick Kipshidze who was practicing in New York at the time, told Sahota, "Harry let's go to Punjab and set up a cardiology clinic there." It was an exciting proposition, and Sahota, in spite of his heavy workload and travels, decided to give the idea a shot. Kipshidze was from the other Georgia—part of the erstwhile Soviet bloc. Sahota and Kipshidze had done a bit of work together in cardiology research on animals. They had even put together medical papers, and had grown to trust each other implicitly. Kipshidze's family was close to Stalin who was Georgian too. Both came from the Tbilisi area, the capital of Georgia. Nick Kipshidze said in an interview that "he strongly believed that Dr Sahota was always ahead of his time by 20-25 years."

Kipshidze wanted to set up a clinic that would combine the best of American and Russian techniques and practices. He was clear that the service they'd provide in Punjab would match up with the same world class standards that they delivered to patients in the USA. Kipshidze and two others travelled with Sahota on at least a couple of occasions to Chandigarh. Kipshidze who in later years became one of the Georgian President's closest confidantes was a man of great intelligence who could easily sense a good opportunity and wanted to grab it. He witnessed Sahota's obvious goodwill in the Punjab capital, the numerous friends that the Indian cardiologist had, and knew that if he could persuade his friend Harry to set up a clinic, it'd be nothing less than an overnight success.

Sahota too saw wisdom in good friend Kipshidze's words, and the big picture that his Georgian-American friend had painted before him. Kipshidze wanted the clinic named Sahota Heart Institute. Sahota became serious about the idea. A place was rented in Chandigarh, and a company by the name of Sahota Heart Institute was registered in Jalandhar, about 95 miles away from the Punjab capital. The deal was that one of Kipshidze's two friends was going to be in Chandigarh full-time to oversee operations, at least during the initial years. He was a Georgian who lived in Moscow. Sahota himself knew that it was not going to be possible for him to stay for lengthy periods in Punjab, after all he had a young family back home in the USA to look after, a roaring practice, and many other professional commitments. So he needed someone reliable to run the show in Chandigarh.

Sahota relied on Kipshidze for providing the supervisory assistance for the new clinic. But Kipshidze, and Sahota, were let down by the man from Tbilisi, Georgia, who after a while refused to continue in Chandigarh. His reasons for backing out were never made clear to Sahota and Kipshidze. Sahota knew that unless he found someone who had worked at world class facilities, and had international exposure, Sahota Heart Institute could not be managed well. Even though he was ready to invest money, finding such a person became quite an ordeal. The man from Garhdiwala had to drop his plans to start what could have been a vibrant business venture in Punjab. But at least he had tried very hard.

Looking back Sahota has a tinge of regret. He knows that if the institute had been opened in the mid 1990s, it would certainly have been the first of its kind in India. Since he was the man who'd done the very first angioplasty in India, his name would have drawn people from a large catchment area. Besides, he had spoken to a firm that had agreed to make balloons and catheters in Mohali, Punjab and supply them not only to the proposed institute, but also to the USA, and South East Asian countries. Sahota could see that the cost of the catheters would have been such that with his considerable contacts he could have supplied them to hospitals across continents, including in North America, Africa, Europe and South East Asia. He believes that he could have sold the catheters by the thousands at half the price that they were then selling in the American markets. "We could have cashed in heavily, and the entrepreneurial adventures would have made us very rich" he says.

Even though he was way ahead of others in practice, somewhere the business skills had not yet set in. Besides, he found nobody suitable in India who could have run his clinic with any degree of efficiency and honesty. It was an opportunity missed, but a lesson learnt. A lesson that taught him that success is not guaranteed in every domain in life. But through his contribution to cardiology in the USA, he gained much recognition, something which he would not have received if he had plunged himself into business in India two decades ago. ∎

MORE TO LIFE
THAN MONEY

Usually it's all about the money. But in the case of Dr Sahota, even though he's been blessed with enough, money has never ruled his life. A double income among doctor couples is common practice. After all, if the spouse is a qualified doctor, she can add to the family income in ample measure by being in a job or in practice. Few such couples think of giving up their double income as the possibilities of growing financially are huge, particularly in the USA where doctors have traditionally done very well.

But Sahota has been an exception to the

The Sahotas did not wish to leave Neil—in this picture two months old in January 1975—with a baby-sitter

rule. His wife Asha is a qualified doctor who was a captain in the Indian Army before she got married. When she arrived in England in December 1972, Sahota had organized a residency for her at the Maelor General Hospital in Wrexham. She worked for just over a year before the Sahotas moved to the USA. In 1974, their first child, Neil, was born in Rochester, New York. It had been decided beforehand that when the child arrived, Asha would stop working. It also meant that the couple was giving up the possibility of doubling their income. As in all the major things in their life, the Sahotas were very clear in their

Sahota at home next to a TV screen that shows the picture of Captain (Dr) Asha Sahota in Indian Army uniform

The famous cardiologist at the entrance to his clinic at 9810, Park Street, Bellflower, near Los Angeles

reasoning. In the absence of family support that is normally available in India, they did not want Neil to grow up in the hands of a maid. Sahota was quite convinced that families in America could be sustained rather well on a single doctor's income, there was no need for two to earn. At the same time he has never been critical of those who have a double income. All he says is that had he been after money, all his decisions in life would have centered around that one single thought process—something that has destroyed the fabric of so many families across the world.

TURNING DOWN A HUGE OFFER

When the Sahotas arrived in Rochester, New York, from England, things were comfortable. Sahota had a doctor's license, he and his wife had legal immigration documents, and the future looked really bright. It was now up to Sahota to shape it the way he wanted, with the choices he'd make. While in England he had written to a few places, including the Regina Hospital in Saskatchewan, Canada, and they had evinced considerable interest in him, just like the one in Rochester had. He took up the offer in Rochester, but promised the Canadians that once he was done with his cardiology training, he'd come to them for about a year.

Somewhere down the line, Rochester threw up an offer that was hard to resist. Back in 1975, the hospital guaranteed him a minimum of USD 100,000 annually, if he continued to stay and work with them. Over some forty years ago, that figure was surely equal to a million dollars today. That's the kind of money no ordinary person would decline. Apart from the money Sahota would get perks and benefits. When an employer wants to pamper you, they throw in several other incentives. He would get an office, assured number of patients, and all the other expenses of staying in Rochester would be taken care of. The hospital management had made a calculated offer, quite certain that Sahota would not refuse.

But Sahota's conscience did not let him down. He politely turned down the offer from Rochester on the grounds that he had a commitment to fulfill in Canada. "If I was after the money, I would not have moved out of Punjab in the first place. And certainly not out of Rochester in the second," he muses many years later, sitting at home in Laguna Beach, California.

B.C. Forbes, the founder of *Forbes* magazine, has said that, "real riches are the riches possessed inside." It has turned out to be true in Sahota's case. After declining the Rochester offer, he took up his assignment in Canada with a package that appeared peanuts in comparison. He agreed to join the Regina Hospital at about USD 800 a month. That worked out less than USD 10,000 per year, a tenth of what the New Yorkers had offered him annually. That he could turn his back to so much money, of course, made him an infinitely happier man, and richer inside. He says that the fact that he could muster enough courage to refuse Rochester hospital's offer was testimony to the family values and strong upbringing that he had in Garhdiwala. "I completely attribute that ability to look beyond money to my parents. I was blessed generously by them with a very wise value system," he says, a hint of emotion running through his eyes.

NO RISK TAKER

Also Sahota realized early in life that he was not somebody who would take undue risks in life. Right from the time he left India, he had made certain that everything before him was in order, he would not let the winds of uncertainty blow his way at all. He did not want to feel uncomfortable running into a situation that could even remotely jeopardize his career, or his family's welfare.

That is why he did not proceed with a company in Punjab which had shown interest in supplying him catheters if he had set up the Sahota Heart Institute in Chandigarh in the mid 1990s. He was too much into practicing modern cardiology, inventing new techniques, and spreading it all over the world. Even though the business prospects of taking up the catheter proposition in India were tremendous, he let it go. As he's admitted, he could have cashed in heavily by selling catheters from India in the USA at about half the price that they were selling in the American market in the mid 1990s. For that matter he would have taken the products to markets across Europe, Africa and South Asia, and made a windfall. But instead he chose the safer road. He wanted to become a top practitioner of cardiology, and by having invented the perfusion balloon, he wanted to stay ahead of the game in his own profession. Risk taking in business was not for him, and making serious money was never the real objective of his life.

In fact Sahota's philosophy was just the opposite, as he constantly veered towards cutting his risks. He knew that he was making a decent living in the USA, and his family was comfortable. He did not want to create a situation where everyone would be on tenterhooks about the outcome of his business. He patented several products including the much talked about perfusion balloon. But when it came to cashing in on his patents,

Asha's parents Mr Niranjan Singh Claire and Mrs Bhagwant Kaur Claire (seated) with Sahota, Dr Nicholas Kipshidze (standing right) who was at the time Director of the Heart Institute in Tblisi, Georgia, and Dr Zulich (standing left), a fellow doctor from Bosnia Herzegovina, at the time part of Yugoslavia. Photo taken at Asha's parents house at 135, Sector 8A, Chandigarh

he was found wanting. In fact some of his patents have been stolen, even after he spent hundreds of thousands of dollars on them, and also in attorney fees in the USA. He had nearly 30 of them, but now they have expired. While the life of a patent was 20 years earlier, now it's been cut down to 17. Once it expires, anyone is free to commercially use the patent. Several companies have used his patented products to start successful businesses. In fact, good friend Nick Kipshidze had warned him thus, "Harry

you wait and see. Once your patents expire, all these companies will start making money from them." Some companies indeed are today. But Sahota himself has not regretted not going into business.

Sahota's explains his lack of interest in commercially exploiting his inventions. "I was happy with having invented the perfusion balloon. I invented something that people are using. There are two companies right now that are making money on two of my inventions. I believe that the patents were created to stimulate invention. If it could be sold by someone, then for me it is an appreciation of the inventor's work, and a compensation of his efforts."

That Sahota thought of benefiting the larger world around him has not gone unnoticed. Someone who's known him closely is San Diego-based Dr Inder Anand who was director at PGIMER, Chandigarh where Sahota performed India's first angioplasty. Anand finds it highly creditable that Sahota flew an entire team along with catheter balloons and equipment from the USA to India to start the angioplasty interventional program in Chandigarh. "He did all those things while he was in private practice, which is even more creditable. In private practice you do not do these kinds of things, because you lose finances as it keeps you away from practice, and does not get you any income. He's a person who has this side to him that wants to help people," Anand says.

His helpful nature and risk aversion have remained Sahota's constant companions throughout his journey. The same aversion to risk kept him away from next door Ireland while he was in England. The IRA was active those days, and Sahota did not feel like going there. Same reason he has avoided visiting "trouble spots" which are not very safe and secure, reason why West Asia, Latin America and Africa have not been on his touring agenda even after so many years. As he has been an avid news reader and watcher, Sahota keeps himself updated with the latest goings on across the world. It is a habit that he formed very early in life, a habit that allowed him to think about leaving India and see some new nations in the first place. "May be it is the downside of reading newspapers. I consider myself a news junkie and so have stayed away from places that have law and order issues," he explains.

As he grew professionally and his name as an inventor of the perfusion balloon spread globally, he received many offers to settle down in different parts of the world. Once after he flew down to Guadalajara, the second largest city in Mexico, to perform the first angioplasty in that country, a noted cardiologist made a Rochester-like offer to him. It was October 1989, and Sahota had also combined his visit with a few lectures along with the procedures. Highly impressed by Sahota's professionalism the cardiologist asked him to settle down in Mexico. Money, house and benefits would be decided as per Sahota's demand. But the offer was declined. Similarly, an entrepreneur who was building a brand new cardiac center somewhere between Chandigarh and Ambala constantly pursued Sahota to join up as the main cardiologist. With benefits and incentives, Sahota knew he could make enough money, but once again stayed away. Likewise, offers came from Russia and Ukraine. But he chose not to rock his professional boat that had been sailing smoothly in the West Coast of the USA.

Even today, at his Bellflower office in Los Angeles, Sahota remains distinctly uncomfortable having to deal with the administrative part of his practice. That includes having to handle staff recruitments, negotiating pay, talking to insurance companies, dealing with changing rules, regulations, laws, contracts, vendors and other non-medical issues. "I love to deal with patients, stay involved with the procedures, and remain focused on my strengths. That is where my comfort levels lie," he says.

As Jonathan Swift the Anglo-Irish satirist who famously essayed *Gulliver's Travels* says, "A wise man should have money in his head, but not in his heart." Sahota, the heart doctor, has walked this ancient wisdom from the day he graduated from Patiala Medical College in 1964. ∎

Harvinder Sahota is forever indebted to his mother for the
valuable lessons of life that she imparted to him

MORALS OF GARHDIWALA

"My morals are important to me"
—Hunter Parrish

For hundreds of years, Sher Shah Suri's Grand Trunk Road has connected South Asia to Central Asia. On the east it starts its journey at Chittagong in present day Bangladesh, passes through West Bengal, makes its way to Delhi and Amritsar, before passing through Lahore and finally ending up in Kabul. Garhdiwala is a 570-year-old town on this famous route. The section of the G T Road where it is located is called the Chandigarh-Jammu National Highway 24, about 18 miles northeast of Hoshiarpur. It is surrounded by the busy townships of Jalandhar, Dasuya, and Talwara.

Garhdiwala remains at the center of commerce, a busy business hub for numerous villages around it. Local businesses here range from pharmacy, electrical and electronic items, cold-chains to wheat storage, grocery, jewelry, clothes, hardware. Its legislative assembly seat is the largest one in entire Punjab. It has been a prolific center of education in the past century. Khalsa Senior Secondary School is the oldest and most famous school of this town and has sent some well-known names from its portals into Government service. Besides, sportspersons from here

have represented India at the international stage. It has also produced great soldiers like Colonel Bachhiter Singh Sahota who laid down his life for the country. Interestingly, Garhdiwala has just over 6,000 people and it does appear that an equal number, if not more, have migrated to countries like US, Canada and U.K. The city bravely endured India's painful partition and managed to bring in a sense of communal harmony to its neighborhoods, even though the same could not be said of several other towns in the region.

History has it that the town was built in 1443 by a Jat named Garhia. The town got a part of its name from him. In 1812, on account of the incarnation of Goddess, a temple was built for her by Jodh Singh, and the town was renamed Garh Devi Wala. A Sardar also built a fort here in 1829, though its remnants are not very visible any more. Around the town are mango groves which go right up till Mahalpur. Eventually the locals settled for the name of Garhdiwala.

It is with the town of Garhdiwala that Harvinder Sahota can associate some of his happiest childhood memories. It is here that he imbibed most of the value system that he's carried with him throughout his life journey. It has enabled him to embrace success. It was at Garhdiwala where his family owned plenty of mango orchards, and his father, Sardar Lachman Singh, once mentioned to his son that there was enough income from the fruits, and that Harvinder really did not have to go abroad to work. Or for that matter leave the town to supplement the family income. Yet, Harvinder Sahota knew that though he would be secure at Garhdiwala, his life was meant to be like an explorer who was interested in discovering the beauty of the ocean, and he would not be content by remaining harbored on the shores. He knew that with his strong family values, he would never attempt anything that could even remotely affect his family's credibility or his father's honor.

He was fully aware that his family had brought him up with utmost care and affection after the near-death incident in his infancy due to double pneumonia. He had received his family's support and blessings to study at the Patiala Medical College, and unlike many families which were far too busy making ends meet, his own childhood and student days had been spent in much contentment. He had made his father proud by becoming a medical doctor, something Sardar Lachman Singh had said he would try and make his son become if he survived the life-threatening pneumonic attack as a baby.

> Likewise, from childhood, he had been trained to respect women around him. He was a shy young man in college. Fellow girl students, to their unending surprise, even found him a bit of a loner, and quite aloof and reserved when he was in their midst

The Sahota household always had enough, and Harvinder was brought up in a secure environment. His mother, Bibi Dhan Kaur Sahota, had instilled deep values in him. They were further ingrained when he had seen the way his sisters had been raised, and that developed in him a deep sense of respect for girls with whom he studied, and for women that he interacted later in life. His mother's love and affection for him instilled in him the real meaning of being committed in life, a laudable characteristic that he has masterfully displayed throughout. His father was an upright railway official—a scrupulous Station Master who had earned the respect of numerous people with whom he had come in contact, and, of course that of his own family and near and loved ones. Sardar Lachman Singh was fiercely honest, and it is a trait that Harvinder has inherited in ample measure, and has never allowed to slip away ever in life. In the larger context of where he is today, and what he's achieved overall in life, Garhdiwala may have been a small town. But even that small town in Punjab trained him to live with honor and dignity in big cities in different parts of the world, in particular places like New York and Greater Los Angeles. It is in such cities where the basic instinct to survive at all costs often undermines the qualities of honesty, commitment and loyalty. Harvinder Sahota retained all these qualities and more and never compromised with them.

It is his sense of commitment that made him decline the offer from Rochester hospital in New York and instead take up a job at one-tenth the salary at Regina in Saskatchewan, Canada. Most people in Sahota's place would have easily fallen for the enticing offer made by Rochester, but Sahota knew that his commitment to Regina meant more to him than all the money Rochester could throw at him. It is a rare and valuable trait that is in exiguous supply in today's world.

Likewise, from childhood, he had been trained to respect women around him. He was a shy young man in college. Fellow girl students, to their unending surprise, even found him a bit of a loner, and quite aloof and reserved when he was in their midst. He was certainly not the most garrulous when it came to conversing with a girl. The coyness was natural and it was combined with a sense of healthy regard for women. While in England when there was no immediate family to keep an eye on him and where he could so easily have misused his freedom, he maintained the same sense of respect and honor when he dealt with women. He did not allow any temptations to come his way, and wrote to his father that he'd marry a girl of his parents' choice, and no other. It is not something that is common any more. In a way he was paying respect to his parents' wishes, more than anything else. Plenty of Indians simply decide to get married to foreign girls in alien lands, once they have emigrated, but Sahota was certainly not the one to follow in their footsteps.

Developing a sense of purpose was always given more importance in the Sahota family than recklessly falling in love with money, or its avaricious accumulation. Had young Harvinder been driven by a desire to amass wealth, he certainly would have insisted that his wife, Asha, work in the USA. After all her income could so easily have bolstered the family's earnings and doubled their purchasing power. Yet, right after son Neil was born in a not-so-inexpensive city like Rochester, New York, a decision was taken that Asha Sahota, a fully-trained medical doctor, would become a full-time stay-at-home mom. Likewise, he gave up lucrative work offers from many parts of the world—like from Russia, India and Mexico. He chose instead to provide more stability to his family when it came to studies for his children, and leading a settled life in the West Coast of the USA. He also thought it prudent that he would hone his scientific and medical skills constantly by developing patents and inventing new techniques in heart surgery, rather than busying himself in marketing his new products and get immersed in the business of filling up his own coffers. If money had been his driving force in life, he could have stayed back in Garhdiwala, opened up a medical clinic, and earned more than adequately from the family's 24 acres of mango orchards. Paul Singh, a businessman from Los Angeles who's known Harvinder Sahota for years, comments on his value system: "Dr Sahota's spoken words are as good as written words. He could have spent a luxurious life. Instead, he is doing so much for uplifting the life of those who are not as fortunate, and they come from all communities."

Like Paul Singh, so many others that know Sahota are able to see that he has avoided allurements that many find difficult to keep away from. While remaining completely focused on raising his own profile in the profession, he's been a family man to the core. He's kept his commitments, and when he commits, it is as though his words are set in stone. It does speak volumes about Harvinder Sahota's grooming and upbringing. Indeed the heart doctor can credit all this to his days in Garhdiwala, a place that effectively helped shape his fine and wonderful value system. ∎

FAMILY,
COMMUNITY AND
POLITICAL AFFAIRS

"Everybody thinks that if you do one thing, you cannot do something else. So I like the fact that I can be versatile if I want to"

—Denise Van Outen

The affable heart doctor is a family man and has travelled widely with Asha and the children. When younger son Eric wanted to study in the East Coast, Sahota accompanied him to several university and college campuses. Finally, Eric decided that he would be a student at the Johns Hopkins University in Baltimore, Maryland. Elder son Neil accompanied his parents to a tour of England in the year 2005 that left both Harvinder and Asha nostalgic with memories of their days in England. The Sahotas have travelled with friends to several places chronicled elsewhere in the book, places such as Las Vegas, Vancouver, San Diego and many more. They have travelled across Europe, but have not made it to the African and Latin American continents. Their own cross-country car journeys in England and America have brought them much joy.

On the community front, the cardiologist has been very busy and he has worked closely and efficiently with friends in the political and social arena. When it has come to fund-raising, Sahota has not been one that has shirked from fronting up. Socially, he remains very active. He is on the Board of Trustees of the World Affairs Council (WAC) of Orange County. In the words of Serge Tomassian, Chairman, Board of Trustees and Executive Board of the World Affairs Council (2016-2017), the WAC is an open forum for Americans to engage in learning and for participating in discussions on world affairs. It remains Orange County's premier forum on world affairs. The Council hosts monthly dinners and luncheons with prominent speakers that include high Government officials, political leaders and global stalwarts, ambassadors and diplomats, journalists, academicians, volunteers, Think Tank experts, among others. The engagements help foster greater awareness and understanding of trending global topics, including geo-politics, regional conflicts, military and defense, economy, national and world security. Council members include former US Ambassadors and diplomats, a diversity of professionals, business leaders, academics, journalists and students.

The Council's Board of Trustees is the backbone of

LEFT: Sahota with President George W Bush and businessman Randhir Tuli during the Presidential campaign of 2003. Bush won and began his second term as US President in 2004. **RIGHT:** Dr Sahota with Indian Prime Minister Narendra Modi at San Jose, in September 2015, a day before the PM addressed a large gathering at the SAP Center. Sahota, pointing to the gathering, asked, "Modi Sahib, all these people from India—doctors, IT people, business people, politicians, movie people, don't you think this is brain drain? The Prime Minister said, "No, I don't call it brain drain"

LEFT: Sahota with Indian Cabinet Minister for Road Transport and Highways, and Shipping, Nitin Gadkari (left), and Nadadur Vardhan on an exclusive yacht in Los Angeles. Sahota asked the Minister, "Why are so many doctors coming from India to the USA?" To which the Minister replied, "It is because there is more money in the USA." The cardiologist said, "But now the whole scenario has changed, there is more money in India."
RIGHT: In September 2004 in New York with the then Indian Prime Minister Dr Manmohan Singh

LEFT: Charles, Prince of Wales, engaged in a conversation with Asha Sahota with Harvinder Sahota listening in at the St James's Palace in the City of Westminster, London, in May 2008. **RIGHT:** Camilla, Duchess of Cornwall, in conversation with Asha and Harvinder Sahota at the St James's Palace in the City of Westminster, London, in May 2008

LEFT: Dr Sahota shares some finer points about angioplasty with the Duchess of Cornwall on May 7, 2008 inside the St James's Palace. **RIGHT:** Dr Sahota shares his knowledge about the advancement of angioplasty with Charles, Prince of Wales, on May 7, 2008 inside the St James's Palace

The Sahotas with Ed Royce, Chairman of the United States House Committee on Foreign Affairs and his wife Marie (first and second from left), and John Boehner (right) during the latter's term as 53rd Speaker of the United States House of Representatives (2011 – 2015)

LEFT: With Nikki Haley, US Ambassador to the UN and a former Governor of South Carolina, and Congressman Ed Royce. **RIGHT:** With Los Angeles County Sheriff Jim McDonnell

LEFT: With Julia Yarmolovych who manages the popular Las Brisas Mexican American restaurant in Laguna Beach. **RIGHT:** Sahota with Sandra Hutchens at a 2009 function at the Bal Boa Club, Newport Beach, to discuss Principles and Politics. Hutchens is Sheriff-Coroner of Orange County since June 2008

LEFT: Sahota with then Indian Ambassador to the USA Arun K Singh (middle) and Dr Srinivasa K J, Consul General at CGI, San Francisco. **RIGHT:** With Avinder Singh Chawla (left), a community leader and businessman on the Board of Sikh Temple, Santa Ana, and Sandra Hutchens

LEFT: (L-R) Douglas Bowman, Devendra Raj Mehta of *Jaipur Foot*, Launa K Wilson of Riverside University, Asha Sahota, Harvinder Sahota in June 2016. **RIGHT:** Dr Sahota presenting an award to singer Ramneek Kaur from Toronto at a musical evening in Orange County in June 2016

LEFT: The Sahotas with Arnold Schwarzenegger, the 38th Governor of California, sometime in October 2006. **RIGHT:** Dr Sahota receives a *Saropa* from Sukhi Dhillon, President, Sikh Temple at Santa Ana, Orange County

(Standing L-R) Sahota, Congressman Dana Rohrabacher, Ajit Singh Randhawa, Congressman Ed Royce, Alexandria Coronado from the Board of Trustees for Schools in Orange County, Councilman Harry Sidhu, Dr Birinder Sahai, Bicky Singh. (Seated L-R) Jaswinder Kaur Sahai, Kanwaljit Randhawa, Asha Sahota

LEFT: Sahota with Joseph Crowley of the Democratic Party in March 2004. Crowley, a Congressman from New York is also the Democratic Caucus Chair. **RIGHT:** Sahota with Ujjal Dev Singh Dosanjh at a function at the Sheraton Cerritos in Los Angeles in January 2002 to honor the family of the very first Indian and Asian Congressman, Dilip Singh Saund. Dosanjh had served as the 33rd Premier of British Columbia (2000 – 2001), Canada, and been an MP in Canadian Parliament (2004 – 2011) including Minister of Health (2004 – 2006)

LEFT: Sahota with Orange County Supervisor (2003 – 2010) Chris Norby in the early years of the 21st century. Norby nominated Sahota for the Chairmanship of the Orange County Medicine Commission. **RIGHT:** Sahota with Somnath Chatterjee who was Speaker of the Lok Sabha, India (2004 – 2009) and Inder Singh, then President, GOPIO International, on June 6, 2005

LEFT: The Sahotas with James Kenneth Galbraith at a World Affairs Council Orange County meeting in October 2008. Galbraith is a professor at the Lyndon B Johnson School of Public Affairs, University of Texas at Austin. His father, John Kenneth Galbraith, was US Ambassador to India when John F Kennedy was US President. **RIGHT:** Dr Sahota with Sardar Tarlochan Singh (center) and Sohan Singh Chaudhary at the Sikh Art Exhibition at the Smithsonian Museum in Washington DC in July 2002. Tarlochan Singh has been a Member of the Upper House of Parliament in India, and a former Chairman, National Commission for Minorities (2003 – 2006)

LEFT: Sahota at a World Affairs Council Orange County meeting with Norman Tanber (left), Hon'ble Judge James Gray (second from right), Chairman, WAC-OC 2017 – 2018, and former Council Chair Yasith Weerasuriya. **RIGHT:** Neil Sahota with Congressman Dana Rohrabacher (left) and Governor Arnold Schwarzenegger (right) in October 2006

LEFT: Sahota with the 45th Lieutenant Governor of California (1999 – 2007) Cruz Bustamante, also a former Speaker of the California State Assembly and a member of the Democratic Party, and Harbhajan Singh Samra, widely acknowledged as the Okra King of the USA. **RIGHT:** (L-R) Close friend Ajit Singh Randhawa, an engineer by profession, Congressman Ed Royce, Dr Sahota, Harry Sidhu, a former Councilman of the City of Annaheim (2004 – 2012)

LEFT: Chancellor, University of California at Irvine (1998 – 2005) Ralph J Cicerone with Sahota in the early 2000s. **RIGHT:** Sahota with Congressman Dana Rohrabacher (middle) and J S Bedi of the India Post News Service, Southern California

LEFT: As an inventor of the Perfusion Heart Balloon, Dr Harvinder Sahota was invited to the 20th anniversary celebrations of angioplasty in 1997 in Zurich. The first angioplasty was carried out by Dr Andreas Gruentzig in Zurich on September 16, 1977. He is seen with other cardiology practitioners. **RIGHT:** With Hollywood actor Ed Asner in the early 1990s at Beverley Hills during the opening night of the screening of the movie *Masters of Success*. It was co-produced by Harvinder Sahota

Smithsonian gathering at Los Angeles sometime in 2004 – 2005 with Paul 'Singh' Taylor (middle). Also seen in the picture with Sahota are Mohinder Singh, Editorial Advisor of India Journal (extreme left), Gurdeep Singh Malik (third from left), Sohan Singh Chaudhury, M Kamboj of Sitar restaurant in Pasadena (extreme right)

LEFT: Dr Sahota with Dr Richard Myler (center), a pioneer in modern interventional cardiology who performed the first coronary angioplasty in a Cath Lab in the USA. Dr Myler was recognized on March 14, 1993 by Sahota at a gathering of world cardiologists in Anaheim. **RIGHT:** Dr Sahota in 2015 with Dr Hazem Chehabi, practicing nuclear medicine doctor and neighbor of the Sahotas at Laguna Beach

Dr Sahota with pioneering heart surgeon Dr Jerome Kay (3rd from left) in 1986.
Also in the picture is Dr Pablo Zubiate (2nd from left), another well-known heart surgeon

LEFT: Sahota embraces the father and son duo of Ed Royce Senior and Ed Royce Junior at Anaheim in June 2006.
RIGHT: Neil Sahota (left) with Dr Carl Clowes, Sahota's colleague from his days at the North Wales
Hospital, and Dr Kundan Singh (right) in North Wales in 2005

(R-L) Daya Singh, Sahota's childhood friend at his home in Amritsar with his son Jatinder, wife Amrik, daughter-in-law Simran, granddaughter Mannat and Whitney Braun, faculty of Loma Lindia University, Riverside, California who was visiting India

LEFT: Sahota with Consul General Mariuz of the Czech Republic, and Dr James Coyle (center) of Chapman University, Orange, California. **RIGHT:** (L-R) Chairman of WAC Serge Tomassian (2016 – 2017) with wife Mona, Dr Parmis Khatibi, former Chairperson (2015 – 2016) of WAC and Dr Sahota

LEFT: Sahota with Consul General Hans Jorg Neumann of Germany (left) and Consul General Eugen Chivu of Romania.
RIGHT: Sahota with Reza Pahlavi II, son of the Shah of Iran, at a World Affairs Council Orange County meeting

LEFT: (L-R) Asha Sahota, Dr Mark Juergensmeyer, Professor of Sociology, Global Studies and Religious Studies, University of Santa Barbara and Serge Tomassian, Chairman (2016 – 2017), World Affairs Council Orange County.
RIGHT: WAC Treasurer and Golden Orange Awardee Errol Mathieu with wife Candace and Asha

(Seated L-R) Saibal Kar, MD, Tarlochan Kler, MD and Padma Bhushan—a high Indian civilian honor, Kusum Chawla, Rajni Dang. (Standing L-R) Sanat Chawla, MD, Harvinder Sahota, MD, Yadavinder Dang, MD and Asha Sahota

LEFT: Businessman Paul Singh (left), Dr Sahota and Mr Venkat from CGI San Francisco. **RIGHT:** (L-R) Dr Jaswant Modi, Dr Sahota, Brian Hervey, VC University Advancement, UCI, Yogesh Shah, Raju Shah

LEFT: Jo Ellen Chatham, Sahota, Jackie Mizani. **RIGHT:** Dr Narender Kapany, widely known as the Father of Fiber Optics, is Chairman of the Sikh Foundation and collector of Sikh Arts and Paintings. Dr Sahota is in discussions with him

LEFT: Dr Sahota with the family of Raj Kamal (middle). Also seen in the picture are Raj's daughter Sushma (left), and (right to left) his wife Sushil, son Dr Sandeep Khanna, Ophthalmologist, and daughter-in-law Nirja. **RIGHT:** Sahota with nonagenarian George Key (center), the great-great grandson of Francis Scott Key who wrote the US national anthem and Young Kim, Assemblywoman from California

LEFT: Charles, Prince of Wales, has things to share with a group that includes Neil Sahota and his father at the St James's Palace in the City of Westminster, London, in September 2010. **RIGHT:** In 2005, the Sahotas visit the smallest house in Great Britain located in Wales

LEFT: In 2010, Dr Sahota visited the Cardiology Department at the Addenbrooke's Hospital, Cambridge University, along with Sir Eldon Griffiths, British Conservative politician and journalist. Here a dinner was thrown in Sahota's honor and he was seated on the central chair.
RIGHT: Sahota presenting a copy of his first biography to New Jersey Congressman Frank Pallone

the WAC, serving a vital role in planning and supporting events through trustee networks and resources. The Board of Trustees is composed of some of Orange County's top business, academic, social and Government leaders. Among them is Dr Harvinder Sahota whose prominence as a cardiologist, social leader, and philanthropist has added immense value to WAC activities.

The County of Los Angeles Sheriff's Department is the largest Sheriff's Department not only in the USA, but also in the world. The department employs over 17,690 persons, patrols over 177 county parks, golf courses, special event venues, two major lakes, 16 hospitals, over 300 county facilities, 10 community colleges. It is also the second largest transit police force after the NYPD. It polices Metro trains and buses of the Los Angeles Metropolitan Authority and *Metrolink,* the latter transporting about 39,000 passengers each day over 534 miles of rail network across Southern California (in comparison, New Delhi Metro network, considered very extensive, transports 2.7 million passengers across 135 miles of rail tracks daily). Harvinder Sahota made a remarkable contribution to his community when on his recommendation a turbaned Sikh was hired in the 1990s by the Sheriff of Los Angeles County as a Deputy. This was quite likely the first such recruitment in the entire USA.

This is how the recruitment was initiated. Sometime in the 1990s, Sahota received a call from the office of the administrator at the Coast Plaza Hospital in Studebaker. The caller said that Sheriff Leroy David 'Lee' Baca was coming and the hospital would like Sahota to come down and meet with him. The cardiologist, however, put down a condition. He said he'd come only if he had the opportunity for a one-on-one meeting with

Dr Sahota speaks to Asha Sahota with Neil by his side in September 2010 in London. They were watching the polo match between a team of Prince of Wales and a visiting Indian one. It was in celebration of *Saragarhi Day*, one of history's greatest last stands (see text for more) on a field of battle

Baca. Eventually, Sahota went to meet with Baca along with Ajit Randhawa, an engineer, and one of two close friends (the other being Balbir Brar) with whom Sahota would walk on the Pacific shores of Laguna Beach. During their 14-year morning excursions amid the cool and fresh drafts of the ocean, the three—Sahota, Randhawa and Brar—left footprints of a special intimate friendship on the sands of time.

There were several people waiting to meet Baca, but just before the general meeting, an administrator at the hospital quietly signaled to the two to move into a side room. When Sahota met Baca face to face, he did not waste time. He handed him over a check, a donation to help him run his next political campaign. Baca did not also pause after he had accepted the check. "What can I do for you Dr Sahota?" he asked. Sahota could have asked for a personal favor, but chose instead to put in a different kind of request. "Sheriff I want you to keep one Sikh with a turban as a Deputy in your department." Baca responded swiftly again: "Get me the man, and he's in." It was a quick quid pro quo, and a turbaned Sikh was hired in the 1990s by the Sheriff of Los Angeles County as a Deputy.

Aside from his sense of occasion, Sahota's sense of

Gathering of Garhdiwala ladies at the house of Kuldip Singh Sahota
in Telford, England, in the year 2005. That is the house where Sahota stayed after
arriving for the first time in England in 1967

history has been immaculate, helping him to develop well-rounded and thought-out world views on various subjects. While in London in September 2010, he did not miss out on the historical *Saragarhi Day*. The Battle of Saragarhi was fought between the British Indian Army and the Orakzai tribesmen in the North West Frontier Province. The army post of the British contingent of 31 Sikhs—then part of the 36th Sikhs and now called the 4th Battalion of the Sikh Regiment—was attacked by around 10,000 tribesmen. The Sikhs led by Havildar Ishar Singh fought valiantly unto death. The day went down as one of the greatest last-stands on a battlefield. Helped by the incredible resistance of so few against so many, another British Indian contingent was able to recapture the post two days later. While in London in September 2010, Sahota along with Asha and Neil made sure to attend a polo match on *Saragarhi Day*—hosted in remembrance of the victory in Afghanistan. The match was played between the Prince of Wales' team and a visiting one from India headed by Dr Pawandeep Singh Kohli, a Radiologist and son of Tarlochan Singh, Member of the Upper House of Indian Parliament and Chairman of National Commission for Minorities (2004-2010). Another team member was

LEFT: Dr Sahota with HWPL Chairman Man Hee Lee and Chairperson of IWPG (International Women's Peace Group) Nam Hee Kim. IWPG is part of HWPL. **RIGHT:** (L-R) Chief Guest Ed Royce, Dr Sahota and Serge Tomassian at the annual function of the Board of Trustees Social of the World Affairs Council. The Social was hosted by Dr Sahota on May 11, 2017

LEFT: Dr Sahota (extreme left) takes part in a program of the HWPL. On extreme right is Chairman Lee and seated next to him is Instructor Ted Moon. **RIGHT:** (L-R) Asha Sahota, Congressman Ed Royce, Harvinder Sahota, Helen Haig, Serge Tomassian at the WAC dinner on May 11, 2017

Dr Sahota attending a meeting of Heavenly Culture, World Peace, Restoration of
Light (HWPL) in July 2016 at Orange County. Instructor Ted Moon (extreme right) and
Bhai Satpal Singh (second from right) are to be seen among other members

one of the grandsons of Captain Amarinder Singh, present Chief Minister of Punjab.

Dr Sahota is also active with Heavenly Culture, World Peace, Restoration of Light (HWPL). Founded in 2012, HWPL has a fundamental goal of achieving world peace and the cessation of war. It has 70 branches in Korea and another 100 branches around the world. With peace and respect for life as its core values, HWPL engages communities across the world in a spirit of love and harmony. HWPL sows the message of peace in all corners of the earth. Here global leaders come together regularly to make a collaborative effort in demonstrating the creative solutions to world peace, solely based on their religious scriptures. Sahota brings in his value system as a cardiologist who is constantly looking for the larger good of people, and trying to maintain peace and harmony in the community by keeping his own moral and ethical standards very high. Whenever he gets an opportunity, Dr Sahota speaks on Sikhism, enlightening the Inter-Faith community on the timeless messages of the Gurus.

He is also one of the respected seniors at the Sikh Temple at Santa Ana, Orange County, where regular meetings take place to ensure that the younger generations born in the USA do not lose touch with their roots, and keep the fires of traditions and festivals burning at all times. ∎

ਮੁੱਖ ਮੰਤਰੀ, ਪੰਜਾਬ

CHIEF MINISTER, PUNJAB

No.CMS-17/203   April 10, 2017

Dear Mr Sahota,

     Thank you for your letter of the 15th March, 2017, congratulating me on my taking over as Chief Minister, Punjab.

2.   The contents of your letter and the accompanying photographs have made me recall the whole day that we spent together in Orange County, California, in May 2016.

3.   I treasure the message and your precious gift, "Hero of the American Heart."

     With regards,

Yours sincerely,

(Amarinder Singh)

Sh. H. Sahota, MD,
(sahotamd@verizon.net)

A TRYST WITH CAPTAIN

"I am the Master of my fate, I am the Captain of my soul"
—William Ernest Henley

By a sweet coincidence, March 11, 2017, the day Captain Amarinder Singh turned 75, also happened to be the day that the election results of five states in India were declared. Amarinder, a Royal and former Captain in the Indian Army, led the Congress party to a resounding victory in Punjab, winning 77 of the 117 seats in the state legislature and was able to celebrate his 75th birthday in style, with much music, fanfare, *band and baja*. He had been entrusted with the charge of the Punjab Congress in November 2015. In less than a year and a half he managed to deliver big time. An electoral triumph by a near two-third majority in Punjab was about the only silver lining in a dark cloud of setbacks for the Congress. The party had disintegrated to near extinction in Uttar Pradesh (managing only 7 of 403 seats), a state it used to rule with much pomp in its heydays. It was routed in Uttarakhand (winning only 11 of 69 seats). Even in Manipur and Goa, the two other smaller states which had gone into elections, the Congress failed to form the Government in spite of winning more seats than its arch rival—Bharatiya Janata Party—because possible allies deserted it. The win in Punjab was, therefore, critical in salvaging lost pride. In days to follow after the victory, Amarinder Singh was to become Chief Minister of the Government of Punjab.

It was in April-May 2016 that Amarinder Singh was in the West Coast of the USA along with several Congress MLAs. The Head of the Royal family of the erstwhile State of Patiala held several meetings in the community. Both at public functions as well as at private dinners he had maintained with confidence that the glory days of Punjab could be restored. He had been telling the Punjabi population in the Greater Los Angeles area on what he planned to deliver if he won and became Chief Minister, and how he would come good on his promises. Dr Sahota attended several of those meetings, some of which were attended by thousand or more people. One meeting was held on May 1, 2016 at the *Swad of India*, a restaurant in Upland in the San Bernardino County, part of California's Inland Empire. Here Amarinder Singh was addressing a group of about 50 Media persons drawn from the Southern California region. Following the press conference,

Harvinder Sahota put his right hand over the Captain's heart and told the Punjab leader that if indeed he could convey to the people of Punjab the same message that he had delivered in California, then he would become the Chief Minister. The points Amarinder made were as follows:

✓ There would be a two-pronged attack to tackle the drug menace. First, oxygen to drug traffickers would be cut off by choking all supply routes. Second, medical treatment would be provided to addicts on a war-footing so that they could become useful citizens again.

✓ Punjab's farmers would be paid the same day that they sell their produce. They were made to wait a month or so before they received their payment, pushing them into debt situations.

✓ Issue of water scarcity would be addressed. It was critical to this farming state. Irrigation had to be improved to revive Punjab's predominance in agriculture.

✓ Industry would be brought back to Punjab. One of the prime reasons that industries had left Punjab was due to the erratic supply of power which direly affected production.

✓ Amritsar and Chandigarh airports would get direct flights from USA, Canada, and European countries. This would not only be convenient for the people of Punjab flying in and out of these countries, but also for those travelling to

With Captain Amarinder Singh in 2016

Jammu and Kashmir, Himachal Pradesh, and bordering areas of Haryana and Rajasthan. It would boost tourism.

✓ Increase the salary of doctors and improve their working conditions so that they do not leave Punjab. The shortage of doctors all over India is to the tune of 800,000.

✓ Restore pride of the youth in the Punjabi language and its vibrant culture so that they revert to speaking Punjabi at home and appreciate their own history and tradition.

Going by the Punjab election results, looks like the wise Captain did take the illustrious Cardiologist's words to heart! ■

Receiving the *India Empire Award for Philanthropy* from former GOPIO International President Ashook Ramsaran at Beverley Hills, California on November 13, 2015

INVENTIONS, RECOGNITIONS AND ACCOLADES

"Invention is a process, you don't get there overnight"

—Louis Foreman

Remember that when only a few days old, Harvinder Sahota had stopped breathing and his family had begun to mourn his passing away? But after several minutes of silence, he breathed again, and this time his family broke down with tears of joy. Ever since that time, Sahota has not let a single breath go waste. He has utilized his time on earth fruitfully, and has accepted with great gratitude the new lease of life that was given him.

It leads us to the inventions that he managed to carry out in spite of his busy and hectic schedule as a doctor. Sahota had just taken up his third year Fellowship in Cardiology at the St Vincent Medical Center in July 1977. A typical problem that doctors had to deal with on a regular basis began to play on his mind. He found that after conducting angiograms, doctors would press the punctured arteries with their hands for several minutes in order to stop them from bleeding. The process was often long and tedious, but nevertheless had to be undertaken for lack of a viable alternative. Sahota's questioning mind began to tick. He started working on a solution that would be efficient, and time-saving. He knew that if the doctors did not use their hands, they'd be free to do other things and better utilize their time.

Finally, he made a breakthrough. He invented the hemostat, a surgical tool used in procedures for controlling bleeding. After the puncture, pressure would be put on a circular metallic object with an ultrasound sensor at its center. The sensor would measure the blood flow from the artery. Optimum pressure would be applied to ensure that the artery was not completely closed, and yet did not bleed. It would do away with the need to use hands to stop bleeding. A flickering light in the hemostat would continue to display the flow of blood. Even its sound could be heard. It immediately enabled doctors and nurses to work on other issues even as they kept an eye on the life-saving hemostat. Sahota went on to patent this product. Some companies did show interest in the device. But given his hectic schedule as a cardiologist, Sahota couldn't commit time to business negotiations. His lack of experience in marketing and promotion also played a part in the device not hitting the market.

Former Prime Minister of India Mr I.K. Gujral presents the Indian Medical Association's
Distinguished Physician Award of 2000 to Dr Sahota at Annaheim in October 2000

But his big moment was yet to come. In April 1980 he flew down to Atlanta, Georgia, to attend the first demonstration of angioplasty by the world famous Andreas Roland Gruentzig, a Switzerland-based German radiologist. Dr Gruentzig was known as the pioneer of the balloon angioplasty. The world's top cardiologists were in attendance to see Gruentzig's demonstrations. During the demonstrations, Sahota noticed that each time a balloon was inflated inside the artery, it would cut off blood supply to that part of the heart which was beyond the balloon. Patients suffered what appeared to be heart attacks, and this inevitably happened during the inflation of the balloon. Apart from suffering from chest pain, there would be changes in blood pressure and EKG, all pointing to an acute heart attack. Sometimes the situation would become so scary that the doctor had to deflate the balloon and pull it out without completing the procedure so that the blood flow could be restored. "When I saw that, it immediately struck me that all was not right. There had to be a way to keep the balloon inflated for a longer time without causing discomfort to the patient before the procedure was completed," reminisces Sahota of those moments when his brain was on overdrive trying to work out a solution.

PATENTS AND RECOGNITIONS

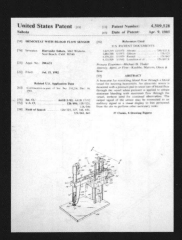

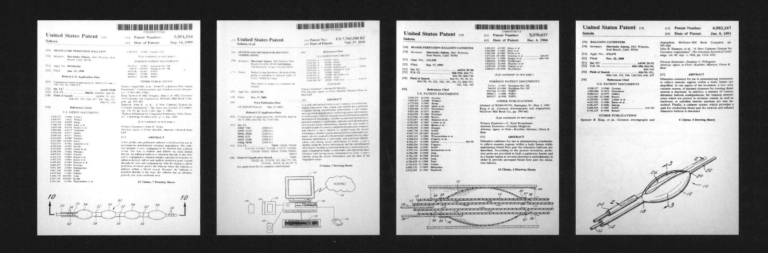

Then suddenly he had his *aha!* moment. He came up with the invention of the perfusion balloon. Along with the balloon arrived fame and accolade in great measure. The perfusion heart balloon would allow blood to continue to flow beyond the inflated balloon and the patient would not suffer a heart attack. He got the product patented.

One day the main catheter company that was building the balloon came to his house at Seal Beach. They wanted total rights to develop and market it. He asked them to go ahead. But barely a month later another firm entered the fray, it wanted the rights too. But Sahota politely declined, saying that he was already committed to another firm. Sahota's negative response did not deter the second company from going ahead with the manufacture of the perfusion balloon and the catheter without permission. It manufactured the product, carried out experiments on animals and then managed to strike a deal with the first company that allowed them to put the product in the market. Requisite approvals were taken from concerned authorities.

The perfusion heart balloon revolutionized angioplasty procedures as it could stay inside the human artery without causing any problem for up to 23 hours. During angioplasty procedures complications do arise occasionally, so open heart surgery is required. But if the hospital has no place for such a surgery, then the patient can safely be transported to another facility which could be hours away, in a different city. The perfusion balloon would ensure proper blood flow to the heart, prevent any attack, and the patient's life would not be in jeopardy. Truly it was a world class product which caught the imagination of businesses in the domain of cardiology.

Sometime later, he and elder son Neil got together to develop a patent on prevention of identity theft through stolen credit cards. It basically meant that someone who got hold of a credit card that was stolen would not be able to operate it since several other security verifications would be required. Overall, Sahota managed to get more than two dozen patents. As of 2017, all have expired.

LEFT: Former Secretary (Medical Education) in the Punjab Government, Mr K K Bhatnagar, IAS, honors Dr Sahota with a special recognition at the 2nd Annual Conference of the Patiala Medical Association in Chandigarh in 1998. **RIGHT:** Indian actress Mahima Chaudhury presents the Global Indian Congress's *Global Indian Award for Excellence in Medicine* to Dr Sahota in San Francisco in 2003

Typically the life of a patent is between 17 and 20 years. After that it can be commercially used by any individual or business without permission. Some of his expired patented products are now doing well in the market.

Somehow business and Sahota never got along very well. The famed cardiologist could not capitalize commercially on his inventions. One of his childhood dreams had been to become an actor, but that had remained unfulfilled. To make up perhaps, he tried his hand in movie production. But the venture ran into financial trouble, as did some other investments he made. Looking back he says, "I realized that for me, business was not the way out. There came a point when I began to concentrate entirely on my cardiology practice. I am happy with my clinic, my consultancy and improving on my skills."

Through all his moments of fame, Sahota remembers his parents fondly. "It was my father's wish that I become a doctor to alleviate the sufferings of others. I also owe the habit of reading newspapers to my father. Wherever he was posted, *The Tribune* invariably arrived at our home. So it gave me an idea of what was going on in the world. And morally, ethically and culturally whatever I am is due to my mother. She told me not to make fun of the physically challenged and not to ever make them feel lesser because of their handicap. My mother was a great soul. She may never have gone to school, but when it came to wisdom she was far higher than most."

On Harvinder Sahota's shoulders rests a wise head, and certainly not without reason. ∎

THE ALMA MATER—
PATIALA MEDICAL
COLLEGE

> *"Medical school education and post graduate education emphasize thoroughness"*
>
> **—Ezekiel Emanuel**

After doing his matriculation from the M.B. Secondary High School in Pathankot in 1957, Sahota joined the DAV College in Jalandhar for his FSc Medical. Having completed that, in 1959 he joined the Patiala Medical College, an institution that was to not only provide him with his Bachelor's degree in Medicine, but also prepare him to face the world for decades to come. This is where Sahota's dreams were shaped, his views strengthened. This is where his ideas found fertile ground to be tested. This is where Sahota for the first time studied in a co-educational environment, something that had been alien to him during his earlier years.

This is also where he forged strong friendships, many of which have stood the test of time.

Patiala is about 45 miles from Chandigarh, the capital of the state of Punjab, and about 145 miles from Delhi, the capital of India. One of its most famous citizens is the Maharaja of Patiala Bhupinder Singh, fabled to be the first Indian to own a car and an aircraft—the Wright brothers' model-B craft. He had a genuine interest in cricket, a game that he himself played with great flair and elegance, and constructed the highest cricket ground in Chail, about 100 miles to the Northeast of Patiala in the mountains of Himachal Pradesh (earlier part of Punjab). His grandson, Captain Amarinder Singh, is a well known politician in Punjab and was the state's Chief Minister for five years between 2002 and 2007. In 2017, he was re-elected Chief Minister of Punjab. He was a captain in the Indian Army. Patiala is also famous for housing the Netaji Subhas National Institute of Sports, considered Asia's fourth largest of its kind. Founded in 1950, the NIS is spread over 268 acres and boasts of several large sporting facilities.

Even though he was shy and reticent, Sahota, much like the name of the annual festival at the Patiala Medical College, had an *aura* around him. In the very first week after he enrolled at the Medical College in 1959, he was unanimously elected Secretary of the student's association. In fact, the subject popped up suddenly when one of his friends, Harbans Singh Dhindsa, said that all the students had decided that he, Harvinder, would become the secretary of the students' body. Shy young man that he

PHYSIOLOGICAL SOCIETY: Harvinder Sahota seated ninth from left was President of the Students' Body at the Patiala Medical College when this group photo of the Physiological Society was taken, sometime in 1960 – 1961

was, Sahota recalls that he was spared the onerous task that year of having to campaign for votes at the girls' hostel. "That year at least I did not have to canvas, and importantly neither did I have to go to the girls' hostel. It would have broken my back, and taking a lot of doing," he says, a large smile breaking across his face some 57 years later. Next year, along expected lines, he was President of the students' body, this time elected. The girls from whom he loved to stay away also, curiously enough, voted for him. They liked his gravity.

Politically quite aware, and abreast with the latest developments in India at the time, Sahota narrates an incident about something that bothers him till date. One day there was a sudden knock on his hostel door. Three boys stood there, and claimed to be carrying out a census survey. They asked Sahota to spell out his mother tongue, to which he replied Punjabi. Likewise they checked with him about the mother tongue of his hostel neighbors Baldev Raj Bhandari from Gurdaspur and Mukand Lal from Delhi. Sahota gave the same response. The boys then excused themselves and went away, saying that perhaps Sahota was busy, and they shouldn't be disturbing him. "I think they were expecting me to say that Hindi was my mother tongue, which I would never have. They left

CME PROGRAM: The alumni of the Patiala Medical College organized the Indo-US Continuing Medical Education (CME) workshop at IMTECH in Sector 39, Chandigarh, India in December 1998. Among those seated are Dr Harbhajan Singh Girgla (second from left), Dr Sahota (center) and Dr Baldev Raj Bhandari (second from right)

because I did not oblige," says Sahota. "There is a good chance that they gave a report to the Census that everyone in Patiala Medical College had Hindi as a native tongue," he says. To him this kind of a survey smacked of a political conspiracy, someone out there was trying to establish that the majority in Patiala, or even entire Punjab, spoke Hindi, and not Punjabi.

It was while he was a student at the Patiala Medical College that the first thoughts of going abroad germinated in his mind. In order to give shape to his desires, he, of course, needed the most vital document that would open the doors to the world outside India—a passport.

One day he was returning to Patiala from his home at Garhdiwala with plans to leave for Delhi the next day in quest of a passport. He had taken a bus from Hoshiarpur, the district's main town some 18 miles from Garhdiwala. At Patiala he came across a shop with a signboard that said "Passport, Visas for England". He went inside to verify whether the documents he had prepared to get his passport were in order. Someone pointed out that the magistrate's stamp on one of the documents was on the "wrong" side. Besides, three additional passport-size photographs were also required. He rushed to a photography shop and got himself clicked. When he asked in how much time he'd get his photographs, the shopkeeper told him to return the next day to get them. Sahota would have nothing of it. He insisted that he wanted the photographs that very day, he had no time to lose. His stubborn persistence paid off, the shopkeeper relented, and in a few hours Sahota's passport pictures were ready.

Then he took a bus back to Hoshiarpur, about 105 miles away from Patiala, and went straight into the court that would stamp his documents. The magistrate did the needful, this time stamping on the "right" side. Within an hour or so, Sahota was back at the bus stop, and by evening he had returned to Patiala. Apart from the over 220 miles that he had travelled up and down on a state highway in buses that were in alarmingly poor conditions, he had managed to get a lot of things done in the course of a single day.

The very next morning he was on his way to Delhi, this time on board a deluxe bus. From the bus stand in Delhi he headed straight to the passport office which he recalls was a decrepit building, with nothing much to boast about. He went up a flight of stairs that seemed to have been swept ages ago, clearly there was no concept of *Swacch Bharat* those days. But the plentiful dust on the staircase was the last thing on his mind. He made his way to a counter and stood before a young Sikh gentleman who told him something that was to warm the cockles of his heart: "Your documents are in order. You can come back here tomorrow and pick up your passport, or alternatively we can mail it to you." Sahota said that he wanted the passport mailed to his home address in Garhdiwala. He then took a bus back to his alma mater in Patiala.

The passport arrived in Garhdiwala within a few days, taking his parents, an uncle and his elder brother by surprise. They had little inkling about what his exact plans were at that point in time. His parents wrote him a letter to inform him about this important development—those days it was difficult to even leave a telephone message at the hostel in Patiala Medical College. Later, passport in hand, Sahota was to buy his ticket to London. And, of course, fledge the nest.

PROUD ALUMNI

Thirty years after he had acquired his passport and flown out of India on an Air India plane, Sahota was in Baltimore to attend

a Patiala Medical College alumni meet in 1997. Actually, he had gone to meet up with Eric, his younger son, who was studying at the time at the Johns Hopkins University, Baltimore. He recalls that it all started over a business meeting on a particular Saturday. The topic of electing the next president of the alumni came up. Someone proposed his name, and everyone present readily accepted. That meant that in 1999 he would be president of the alumni, and it was his responsibility to put together a function at a destination of his choice. It was his prerogative to choose his own cabinet—the team that he'd work with to organize and deliver the event. The first thing he did was

VOLUNTEERS' CORNER: The Patiala Medical College alumni team of volunteers from Southern California that worked very hard to make the 1999 alumni meet at the Laguna Cliffs a grand success

PRESIDENTIAL ADDRESS: Dr Sahota, President of the Patiala Medical College Alumni Association, speaks to the audience at Hotel Laguna Cliffs, Dana Point in the Fourth of July week in 1999

to look out for Patiala graduates in the Los Angeles area. He would build his team around them, and then entrust them with responsibilities of organizing the event. He wanted to make it an absolute success, and in his mind he knew that it entailed plenty of discipline and hard work. Once he had tracked down the alumni members that he needed to work with, he invited them over for dinner, and allocated them tasks and portfolios. The planning for the alumni meet of 1999 was well on its way. Sahota had nearly two years to deliver.

Sometime in 1998 he was required to attend an alumni meet because the following year he'd be in charge. Some loose ends needed to be tied up. That meeting took place under ideal circumstances, on a cruise from the beautiful beaches of Miami to the exquisite shores of the Bahamas. It was also the president-elect's prerogative to choose a location for the alumni meet. Sahota did not waste much time in zeroing in on his choice, it had to be somewhere in Southern California, and it had to be out of the ordinary. The venue selected was the world class Laguna Cliffs Marriott Resort and Spa at Dana Point Hotel, barely 10 miles from the new Irvine Cove house where the Sahotas had moved into in 1997. The hotel has a large meeting and outdoor event space, pools and a number of ocean activities with a bluff overlooking the Pacific. One thing was certain, Dana Point would turn out to be the perfect getaway for the alumni members who'd come from different parts of the world.

Tom Newberry, the well-known American football guard would say, "If you want to lead an extraordinary life, find out what the ordinary do—and don't do it." From past experience, Sahota knew the kind of stuff he wanted to avoid. He remembers, not very fondly, landing up at an alumni meeting in the early years where the president had made no arrangements. There was not even a venue in place, no hotel reserved for those who'd come to the meet, no program drafted. It was a disaster. Only five people ended up attending that particular alumni meet. The next few years were no better.

Sahota knew what he did not want, a repeat. At the time he became president-elect, there were around 1,200 overseas alumni of the Patiala Medical College in the USA alone, plus some more in Canada, and other countries across Europe and Asia-Pacific. He made it clear to his cabinet that things had to change, and drastically. He networked with the alumni and enthused them to attend the event. He also started a news magazine called PANI 5, named after the five rivers of Punjab. Sahota had always been a good leader, and once again his leadership skills came to the fore. Discipline was key to making the event a success. Everyone in his team had to show up at least once a month for a review meeting, and come ready with feedback on all that had been discussed. Plenty of boxes needed to be ticked, the task was not easy. With Sahota around, nobody could take things lightly. Not at least until D-day arrived, and the dance floors were opened up to the alumni at Dana Point.

PANI 5 brought out by Sahota when he was President of the Patiala Medical College alumni association

"The bottom line was that a lot of hard work was involved. Each one in my team took things very seriously, and it was my job to ensure that they all stuck to a game plan. We wanted to set an example, and I wanted the alumni to know that if a president really wanted to create a good event, it could be done. It was not about the position of president itself, but what you did with it that counts," he says.

GREAT SHOW

Eventually the alumni meet was held over the Fourth of July weekend that commemorates the signing of American Independence. It was a four-day weekend that started on a Thursday. Over 600—the highest number ever—attended the alumni extravaganza held on the beautiful Pacific front Dana Point Hotel. Typically, attendance would be between 150 and 250 for alumni meets. Sahota's charm and powers of persuasion, his team's hard work and meticulous planning, and the prospect of enjoying the California weather had all combined to draw people to Dana Point. There were lectures, networking cocktails, gala luncheons and dinners. Equally, there were plenty of opportunities to relax, enjoy the spas, spend time on the lovely beach, compete in a few rounds of the golf green, and swing a few tennis racquets. Doctors and their families came from not just USA and Canada, but Europe and India as well. The Laguna Marriott was full, and happening.

One of the highlights of the Dana Point meet was that Sahota managed to end up with a surplus of USD 50,000

DOWN MEMORY LANE: Seventeen years later Sahota visits the Dana Point Hotel in August 2016 and has fond remembrances of the alumni meet of July 1999

Medical College, and needless to say the management at Sahota's alma mater was more than pleased with this act of generosity.

To keep things from running out of hand, Sahota had independent American security at the alumni meet. Nobody could come in without a ticket, and it applied to one and all. There were those who tried to barge in, but cut a sorry figure. "Some people had not confirmed participation, left no RSVP, had not paid a dime, and yet they wanted to get in. I would have nothing of it," he recalls. When they were turned back, they expressed their ire in no uncertain terms, and have not forgotten the snubs even today. Some of them had flown all the way from England, expecting freebies at the alumni meet. That he could actually turn away alumni who came from England speaks volumes about Sahota's determination to stick to his game plan and discipline.

The ones that did get in, though, had a whale of a time over those four days. They thoroughly enjoyed the hospitality, the arrangements and the leisure activities. The cool Pacific breeze was always blowing their way to make their stay even more pleasant. The sound of the ocean waves rushing back to sea made for pacifying background music.

In successfully organizing the Patiala Medical College Alumni Meet of 1999, Sahota had displayed the thoroughness that Ezekiel Emanuel, the well known Oncologist talks about. It's a trait that he has displayed in ample measure, in every stage of his distinguished life. ∎

in the alumni association kitty, after all expenses were paid for. Monitoring had come easy to Sahota from his childhood days, he had been class monitor in school many times. Here too he closely monitored the expenses, and kept a tight watch. Alumni money was not spent on doling out favors to friends and relatives, all prices were negotiated professionally. Even though fees were raised, more life memberships came in. The USD 50,000 surplus was spent on renovating the auditorium at the Patiala

EVERY DAY JOURNEY—MUCH FOOD FOR THOUGHT

Sahota's mind is fully alert and his thinking cap is totally on as he drives four times a week between his beautiful home in Laguna Beach overlooking the Pacific Ocean and his busy office in Bellflower, and back. During the roughly 50-minute drive, it's a pleasure to hear his deeply analytical views on the world, on India, and on Indians in America. He has an extraordinary understanding of all that's going on around the world because he reads up news from many sources, and flips through several news channels, and knows the ones that are biased, and the ones that are neutral, and the ones that are courageous enough to write and show things as they are. The last category of news purveyors, of course, is a small minority on the verge of extinction. But Sahota, the self-confessed news junkie, will tell you which particular piece of news was covered in five different ways by ten different journalists, because there's always an angle, and a larger objective, political, diplomatic, business and otherwise. He rarely misses out on the top stories around the world, and loves to keep himself totally abreast of the latest happenings in India.

For some reason he prefers the drive on I-405 instead of the more scenic CA-1, the Pacific Coast Highway that gives a magnificent view of the Pacific Ocean on the West. It is also known as the El Camino Real, an old route once traversed frequently on foot by Catholic missionaries from Mexico to Northern California, and beyond. It is on this highway that they would take rest, eat, and move on.

As his BMW rolls out of his home in the pretty and exclusive neighborhood of Irvine Cove in the City of Laguna Beach, the rolling San Joaquin Hills start showing up on the right. And so does the sprawl of the University of California at Irvine—a place where he has set up a Chair for Sikh Studies in the name of his mother Bibi Dhan Kaur Sahota, and also where his elder son, Neil, graduated from.

As we go past UCI, Sahota's memories go back to his own student days. He is now narrating an anecdote. He had just completed his fourth grade at the Khalsa Primary School in Govindgarh, Jalandhar City, and as was the norm those days, had joined the others at Khalsa High School to attend fifth grade. He recalls his very first day in class at high school. The teacher came in, and almost immediately

With Security Officer Lon at the gate of Irvine Cove where Sahota lives

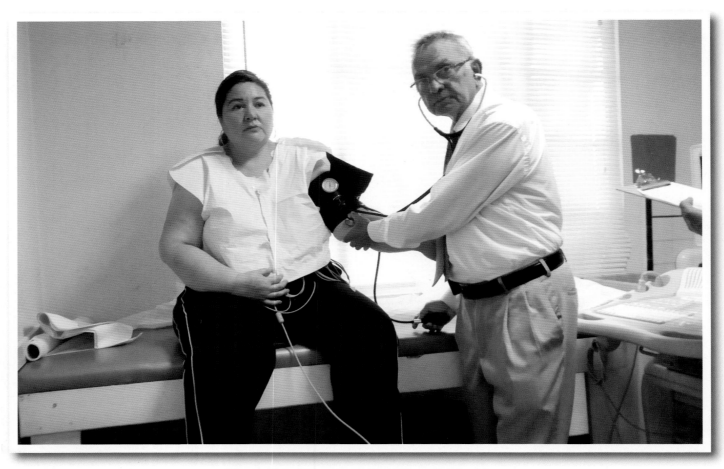

His day has started, a patient has checked in

announced that his first job was to find a class monitor. It was uncanny, his eyes fell on Harvinder sitting in not too prominent a place in the classroom. Pointing at him, the teacher announced that the boy in the blue shirt would be the monitor from that moment on. That was it. No discussions, no consensus, no other selection process was required. Sahota had to look at his shirt to confirm the color, he was surprised at the teacher's speedy decision making. He says, "I am very thankful to God that such incidents occurred in my life." He was to attend the school

for only another month, though, as his father moved them back to Ferozepur cantonment. Interestingly, even at the Government High School in Ferozepur, he was made class monitor. At the Municipal Board High School in Pathankot—now known as the Government Higher Secondary School—which Sahota attended later, he was elected Secretary of the students' body while in ninth grade. Then in the tenth grade at the same school, he became President of the students' body. At the Patiala Medical College, in the very first year he was elected

Sahota tops up his BMW at the gas station next to his yellow office building (on the right side of picture) on Park Street Bellflower

unanimously as Secretary of the students' body, and the next year as President. Clearly, his leadership skills were spotted not just by his teachers, but fellow students as well. Rightly, he credits all these things to God.

A bit further down the I-405 is the John Wayne airport on the right. It is named after one of Hollywood's more enduring heroes of yesteryears and Sahota speaks about the airport's advantages. It is nearer his home, unlike the airport at Los Angeles which is almost 90 minutes away. Also, it is well connected to all major cities in the USA.

Further down the Interstate is the City of Santa Ana on the right. It is the capital of Orange County, popularly referred to as the richest county of the richest state in the richest country in the world. And now he turns his attention to doctors, about whom he has made plenty of analyses. He remembers reading in a journal in the mid-1990s that before starting a business, or choosing to join a particular industry for work, plenty of research is done. Another news report said that white American boys who were on top of their class and would under normal

In August 2016 at the Sikh Temple at Santa Ana next to the *Nishan Sahib*, symbol of Sikh Religion

circumstances have chosen medicine as their first choice were no longer opting for medicine as a career. That is because their research and information showed that there was no future in medicine.

So where were they headed? It was reported that the majority were getting into finances or going into business. The research was right on the money, those who ventured out into the financial world were earning handsomely. Some of them were getting millions of dollars in bonuses in the financial sector. "That is how they go about it in the USA," Sahota says, "with plenty of research to back their decisions." But in India it is like *bhedchal*… implying if one sheep goes in a particular direction, the rest of the flock follow suit, sheepishly, of course, without a thought. Likewise, if one person becomes a doctor, everyone in his family and friends circle wants to tread the same path. One doctor comes to the USA, and everyone wants to come here, without realizing that the profession of medicine has changed, and doctors no longer have the same kind of incomes as before. There is absolutely no guidance, no research, and quite clearly the decisions are not thought through.

One day after he had read that nine in ten American doctors did not wish to send their children to medical school, Sahota asked an American colleague who was white about the reason for this. He also pointed out that white American doctors were retiring early, or were quitting the profession. Pat came the response: "Dr Sahota it is not about the money, although it is important. These doctors find it insulting that after spending lot of time on patients when they suggest a procedure (test) like EKG or Echo, they have to get the permission (authorization) from the insurance companies. Frankly, they find that quite insulting because it is they, the doctors, who have spent so many years studying and training in medicine. Ultimately someone who does not know anything about the patient is getting to decide about the procedure and test."

Sahota then spoke about another report in a medical journal that he had come across in February 2017. It was titled, "Doctors don't love being a doctor anymore". The article according to Sahota had taken the joy out of being a physician mainly because they were now stuck in the quagmire of paper work, rules and regulations such as EHR (Electronic Health Record), MICRA, PQRS, QAPI, ACA, ICD-10 and insurance audits. This phenomenon, combined with reduced incomes, were forcing doctors away from the profession. To compensate for the reduced incomes, doctors were trying to see more patients, which meant that quality time spent on a patient was decreasing. "Look, the media in the USA, and in India, is equally shy of writing these things," says the cardiologist, eyes fixed on the busy freeway ahead.

On the right is the City of Westminster, and much beyond it in the distance is the City of Anaheim, home to the Disneyland Park. As he changes over to the carpool lane to beat the traffic, Sahota brings out another aspect.

He points out medical centers across the USA are in fact trying to reduce their dependency on doctors by shifting the workload to nursing specialists, and allocating more responsibility to physician assistants and maids. This has ensured that the dependency on doctors has been reduced, and shortage, if any, is taken care of. In fact, when it comes to doctors, it is more a case of mal-distribution. There was an oversupply of doctors in large cities. The shortage was in the isolated farming states. Doctors from India who didn't find opportunities in the cities were now forced to branch out to the small towns in farm and rural areas in the sparsely populated states in the Mid West.

Another huge change has been in the income of doctors, a subject Sahota has gone into deeply. Having spent over 40 years in the USA during which time he has been managing a busy medical office, practicing cardiology, reading up medical and research journals, Dr Sahota knows the economic pulse of the market. The average take home income of a doctor these days, according to studies, he points out, is somewhere between USD 10 to USD 25 per hour. "Certainly it is not good enough for a doctor with a family of four to survive in a big city. Quite different from the time when I came to the USA," he says, leaving a few cars behind.

It's now about 10 minutes from Bellflower, with the City of Lakewood on the left and the City of Cerritos and the City of Artesia on the right. Artesia's famous Pioneer Boulevard—referred to as the *Little India* of Los Angeles—is the popular Indian shopping area where many an Indian entrepreneur has made a name for himself. Among others, there are several famous jewelers, grocers, restaurateurs out here. He is still on the subject of doctors. "It is a shame that at a time when India has a shortage of hundreds of thousands of doctors, so many of them are leaving India and going overseas. The Government needs to find a way to stop them," he says. Once an Indian

LEFT: Iqbal Singh, Dr Sahota, Mr Narinder Singh Mahal and Manmeet Singh. **RIGHT:** With Dr Jasbir Singh Mann, Orthopedic Surgeon who is the President of the Sikh Temple at Santa Ana

politician who was visiting the USA from Punjab, said that if all the Indian doctors in Britain were to leave, the health care system in that country would collapse. Another time, in 2016, when a well-known senior Indian cabinet minister was in Los Angeles, Sahota asked him why doctors were in a rush to leave India, even though the shortfall was to the tune of about eight hundred thousand? The minister's response was that doctors were leaving India because they made more money in the USA. Needless to say, Sahota did not find any humor in that statement. At another time when he met Prime Minister Modi in San Jose, he wanted to know why so many doctors, IT engineers, business people, politicians and their families, and Indian movie actors were leaving India and coming to USA. He asked if it was brain drain. The Prime Minister answered that he did not call it a brain drain.

Sahota is now pulling up at the parking lot at his clinic on Park Street, Bellflower, conveniently located next to a gas station. Patients are waiting, and there are several instructions that need to be passed on to the staff, and numerous discussions that need to take place with his doctor colleagues. He needs to go to a hospital or two, as well. The day is just starting out for the evergreen cardiologist. ■

BELLFLOWER CLINIC AND A VISIT TO LAKEWOOD

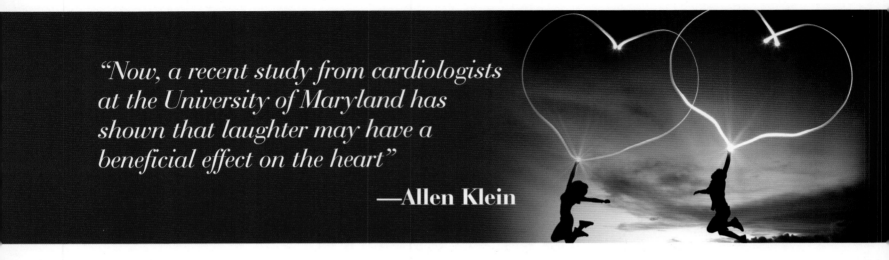

"Now, a recent study from cardiologists at the University of Maryland has shown that laughter may have a beneficial effect on the heart"

—Allen Klein

As a cardiologist, because of all the inventions he has done starting with the impactful and acclaimed perfusion heart balloon, because of all the countries he visited when his legs were younger, because of the first-time angioplasty procedures he performed at various places around the world, including India, because of his innate ability to state things as they are without confusing, because of the number of hospitals that wanted his services and still do, Harvinder Sahota is in a league of his own.

We will read in the next chapter what Dr K.V. Srinatha, his partner of over three decades, thinks of him. Some of his peers have been more than just glowing in their praise about Sahota. They also say that if the staff thinks well of you, then you must be doing things right. Sahota's colleagues indeed have great regard for him. They see in him a mentor, a guide, and also a philosopher who imparts lessons he's learnt from his readings and his intercontinental experiences.

Dr Indy Gujral joined Sahota's Bellflower Clinic in 1996. He had moved to the USA in 1987 after passing out of the Amritsar Medical College in Punjab. He met Sahota at an American Heart Association conference in New Orleans, Louisiana, and managed to keep in touch with the famous cardiologist. When the opportunity presented itself, he joined the team at Bellflower. With over two decades at the clinic, Indy has seen things go from strength to strength. "Dr Sahota is a superb clinician, and a cardiologist. I've learnt a lot of things working with him, and I guess learning is an ongoing process. My learning has not been restricted to cardiology itself, but outside it as well, as in how to better relate to patients and the world at large. Each day you interact with Dr Sahota, you gain something, and it helps build your confidence. He's helped me grow as a cardiologist," he says.

Sahota is one of 20 clients that Rachel Rodriguez has. Her firm, Raedar Medical Billing, does his invoicing for patients, insurance and other companies, and collections as well. She met Sahota through Indy and has worked with him for four years. The one thing that has helped her grow is Sahota's eagerness to share. "Dr Sahota has enhanced my business because he shares information. This isn't

(L-R) Rachel, Tatiana, Marnie, Marie, Sergio, Dr Sahota

With Alma

With Indy Gujral at his office.
Indy joined the Bellflower Clinic in 1996

With Sunny Saran at the Bellflower Clinic in July 2016.
Sunny works with Dr Sahota to set up the Electronic
Health Record that will make the Bellflower Clinic
paperless and help in digital communication with
pharmacies, laboratories, hospitals and other doctors

information that I get from the outside, because it is specific stuff that comes only from a doctor. This is information that I do not get elsewhere. He's been very giving, nurturing. He does not play. He does not cheat. If a competitor comes, he'll tell me what the competition is doing." It has helped Rachel get better at her business, something she's been carrying out for 30 years now. "He's also on top of his work, very thorough, very alert," she adds.

Sunny Saran from Anantapur in Andhra Pradesh, less than 135 miles from Bengaluru, India's Silicon Plateau, moved to the USA about 16 years ago. Torrence-based Sunny set up his business in IT-enabled services for the

Outside the Lakewood Regional Medical Center

health care sector in 2010, and Dr Sahota became one his earliest customers. Sunny's firm manages electronic health records and patient data for the Bellflower office. The incisive feedback he's received from time to time from the cardiologist has immensely helped him grow. Today Sunny has eleven fulltime people drawn from health care, nursing, public health and medical backgrounds working for him. He knows Sahota is a stickler for disciplined work and indeed very thorough in his practice. He's also constantly benefited from the kind heart and generosity of Sahota. "He is one of the kindest persons I've come across, always ready to give great feedback about the work we do with

With Dr Isaac Eisenstein (second from right) and the technical support team inside the Cath Lab at Lakewood

quality and regulatory compliance. Despite the demands of the job, he treats you very well."

Sergio Hernandez who came to the USA from El Salvador, Central America's smallest nation, when he was 10-years-old is a Nursing Practitioner. He trained at the Bellflower Clinic in August 2016 before setting out to prepare for his certification examination. He got to know Sahota well. "Every time I have come in here, I've learnt so much, not only about medicine but other aspects of life as well. Getting to know Dr Sahota was really interesting. He's

really an educated man, and so well informed about things around him. He's been in cardiology for decades, and has tons of experiences and his achievements are exceptional. I'm so lucky that I came here," Sergio observes.

Marie Cruz, Marnie Hernandez, Alma Alcantar, and Tatiana Garcia, have worked with Sahota closely, both at the back and front ends in office. Marie is the most recent entry at Bellflower, having joined just about a year ago. What started off as an extension from school turned into a fulltime job for her at the clinic. She works mostly at

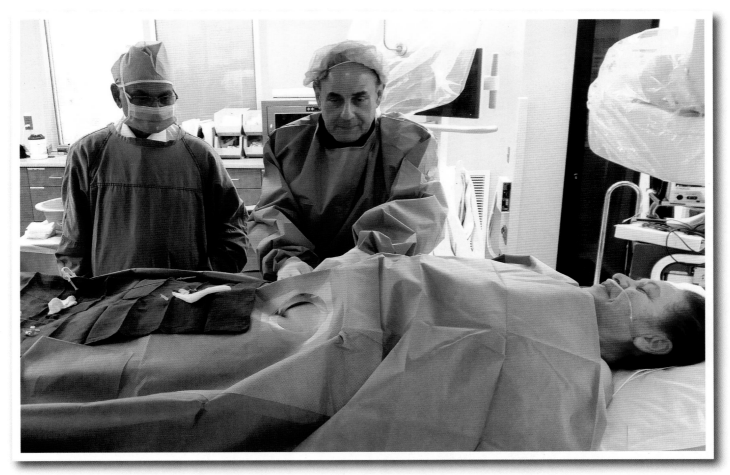

At Lakewood with Dr Eisenstein and a patient ready for surgery in the Cath Lab

the back office, but sometimes she gets involved in the front as well since there is a rotation policy. She's called in to interpret for Hispanic patients who do not speak English, and has seen from up close why Sahota has built such a name for himself. Says Marie: "You have respect for him. He's been an inventor. He doesn't hide facts from patients, he tells things as they are. He tells you the truth, upfront. He's straightforward. Patients prefer doctors who tell it to them at the outset. He then works with his patients to ensure that they put their health first, ahead of everything else."

Marnie is brief, but to the point. She's been around long enough to see Sahota cut down his heavy workload by half. While earlier the doctor from Laguna Beach would drive down to work five days a week, and work through the day, now he comes in four times, and leaves by lunchtime. He's also reduced his hospital visits. Marnie says her work is not at all stressful, and she enjoys every moment spent at the clinic. She works with Dr Sahota when patients come in, interpreting at times, and handling the busy front office

With Dr Paul Yoon whom he's known for nearly four decades at the doctor's dining room in Lakewood

work. And then she pores over medical records, and puts them up before Sahota so that he can analyze and appropriately act on them. "He's so very straightforward, and tells it as it is. It is always a good thing, you know, patients like that. They want to hear the truth about themselves," she says.

The year 2016 was Alma's third year at Bellflower. She was an extern here initially and eventually got absorbed at the clinic. "Dr Sahota can be strict, but he is soft too," she says with a smile. "Yes, he could be a little bit picky, but you know it is all for the best. Patients and staff know that alike. He knows such a lot about the world around him. I've personally learnt so much of history from him. It has made me well-rounded and better informed. In spite of his high caliber as a medical doctor, the one thing he's never lacked is humility," adds Alma.

Tatiana points out that the amount of time that Sahota spends with patients goes to show how much he's really involved. "Probably he spends more time with patients than most doctors would," she says. Tatiana who's put in four years at the Bellflower Clinic has seen a mix of ethnicities walk in and out of the clinic. Indians, Sri Lankans, Mexicans, Hispanic, African Americans form the bulk of his patients, apart from white Americans, of course. The work environment is really healthy and geared towards getting better with each passing day. To all his patients, Sahota is more than just a cardiologist: he brings in his knowledge, his research, and so much more. "He is ever willing to share his global experiences so that we can adequately learn from them, and we respect the fact that he brings so much to the table," she adds.

Indeed he does. Whether it is at the operating table, or a round table for discussions on the world at large, Sahota is forever leading from the front. ∎

A BROTHER
NAMED SRINATHA

"When someone shows you who they are, believe them the first time"
— Maya Angelou

No chapter in Sahota's life will be complete until he mentions the name of Dr K.V. Srinatha. Aside from his immediate family, this is the person with whom Sahota has spent the most amount of time and possibly the most productive period of his life in the USA. They have been together for 36 years, and their friendship has blossomed beautifully into deep brotherly affection, with Sahota, almost a decade older than Srinatha, playing the part of elder brother to perfection. And through thick and think Srinatha has stood by him. A man from India's north, and another one from the country's deep south, have been able to forge together a precious but unlikely bond in America's West Coast that no agreements on paper could possibly have.

Truth is stranger than fiction. Would you believe it?—there is not a single written agreement between Sahota and Srinatha, even though they have been practicing together as partners for well over three decades. Well, it's way too late to draft one anyway. Sahota puts things in perspective. He says that he is not against any written agreement per se, but only if it is followed in letter and spirit. Otherwise, an agreement is nothing but a piece of paper, really. Sahota elaborates on this crucial point: "I'm against such agreements, because after writing, after signing, it doesn't stop both parties to be in court the next day. The same attorneys that have drafted up the so-called 'agreements' and have found them in perfect order one day, will refuse to agree on their contents the next day, picking holes and interpreting every line in their own, different ways."

The illustrious inventor of the perfusion heart balloon says that if two people can trust one another implicitly, do not forget what they talked and discussed, do not have ulterior motives, then really there's no need for an agreement. But if the trust is missing, then it is always better to draft up agreements.

Being in a comfortable space with one another is important, and Srinatha has allowed Sahota that. Over time, they have not just evolved as skilled cardiologists, they have grown spiritually together as well. When the

THEN AND NOW…
With Dr Srinatha at 9810 Park Street, Bellflower, Los Angeles some years ago…
and inside a cabin at the same address in August 2016

two started out on June 8, 1986—on younger son Eric's eighth birthday—Sahota was already a well-established name in cardiology. He was generating handsome revenues from the procedures he was carrying out, and was the only cardiologist at the time doing angioplasty. But he did not hesitate to offer Srinatha, ten years his junior, an equal partnership in the firm. When the question of a written agreement, possibly running into dozens of pages, arose, both decided that they'd have nothing to do with it. A few attorneys occasionally reminded them on whether they had things sorted out in writing, but to their surprise received no answers in the affirmative. All Sahota and Srinatha would tell them is that they had an oral agreement, which was a gentleman's one. "I can bet you that if there had been a written agreement between us, our relationship would not have flowered, it may not have allowed us to grow and evolve," says Sahota.

Srinatha had come to the USA in 1975. After partly training in New York, he moved to California. He is from Mysuru, nominated year after year as India's cleanest city. Growing up, he attended the Mysore Medical College and then went to Pondicherry to do his MD. But midway he pulled out and left for the USA. For him working with Sahota has been an experience he would never have dreamt of while in India.

No doubt he has a great deal of respect for Sahota, one of the several reasons why the partnership has been able to stand the test of time. "For two cardiologists, staying together is not easy. It is like being together in a marriage. We have to be understanding of each other, have a great deal of respect for the work we do, trust one another. If those things are missing, we would not be here today. It is not just a business partnership, we are spiritual brothers," he says, a beatific smile lighting up his face.

Indeed the brotherly affection they have for one another is quite evident as they open up candidly. Srinatha looks up to Sahota not just as a highly respected professional, but also as an elder brother. He knows Sahota too looks at him like a younger brother. They have learnt from each other, and fed off each other's talents and skills. Suggestions are valued, and knowledge is exchanged almost on a daily basis. Srinath says, "I will tell you the truth. He is very good, very intelligent, very inventive. Not just professionally, but even otherwise, socially for instance. He delves deep into issues. He's into religion. He recently learnt about Jainism and gave a talk in front of something like 5,000 people at an international conference in Texas. He spoke on Sikhism and Jainism and highlighted the commonalities. That's how thorough he gets with what he's researching," says Srinatha.

In 1987, a year after they had began practicing together, a huge tragedy was to bring Srinatha and Sahota closer together. Srinatha lost six in his family, including his parents, his brother, sister and two nieces, in a road accident in South India. It turned his life upside down. He was especially close to his brother, an engineer—the two were fondly addressed as Ram and Laxman. "I returned to the USA a shattered and broken man. It was then that Harry told me, 'you know Sri, I know you've lost your brother, but you've not lost hope, because I'm your brother.' He has fulfilled that promise, one hundred per cent. He has truly been my brother," Sahota's partner of nearly four decades says.

Maya Angelou's words sit perfectly on both the well-known cardiologists. They decided to believe each other the first time they met. And blessedly, they haven't had to look back since. ∎

NANCY AND ELAINE— NEIGHBORS TO REMEMBER

I rvine Cove is an exclusive gated community in the City of Laguna Beach in Orange County, southeast of downtown Los Angeles. The beautiful houses in the community have their own private beach overlooking the calm and breathtaking Pacific Ocean. It is one of two such wonderful, exclusive beaches in entire California, possibly in the entire USA. On one of these beaches, popular American shows like Baywatch have been shot.

Most people have their second or third homes at Irvine Cove, so they do not live there throughout the year. Getting to know neighbors, therefore, is not the easiest of jobs, they are hardly to be seen! Given, however, Harvinder Sahota's gregarious nature, and Asha Sahota's affable demeanor, the couple makes friends easily. They entertain guests quite often and their friends usually come away happy after a visit to the Sahota house.

One such neighbor is Nancy Lusk who lives across the street from the Sahota residence with husband Mike. The Irvine Cove house is not their only one—the couple has a few in Southern California, in the Bay area and in Vancouver. They got acquainted with the Sahotas sometime in late 1998 and over the years the acquaintance has developed into a warm, stable friendship. Nancy playfully describes Dr Sahota as her son, and evidently the two get along very well. Mike and Asha, both more reserved, are good listeners. Whenever the four meet up, there is much friendly banter, and views on affairs of the world are freely shared.

Nancy recalls that she came in to Irvine Cove about a year or so after the Sahotas had themselves moved in to this scenic neighborhood sometime in 1997. They had exchanged hellos and smiles from across the street, but were yet to meet formally. One day, though, back in 1999, they surprisingly found themselves sitting across the table from each other at a luncheon hosted by a trust. "As we sort of looked across the table at one another, we figured that we were the same neighbors across the street. It was really funny, and we all started laughing," says Nancy, rolling back the years to a time when Irvine Cove was just about filling up with people.

She liked Sahota's instant wit, and sense of humor.

CURRENT NEIGHBORS: Mike and Nancy stay right opposite the Sahotas and there is no shortage of warmth and camaraderie when the two neighbors meet

NEIGHBOR FROM SEAL BEACH: Elaine Stovee was the Sahota's neighbor for almost two decades at Seal Beach, until they shifted to Laguna Beach. She is now in an Assisted Living complex

While the memories of the conversations she had with the Sahotas are a bit jaded, the feelings she had after the first meeting are still quite vivid eighteen years later. What struck her was that the Sahotas were fun people to be with, and she knew then that this would be one couple they'd like to see more often. Considering that Nancy had slowed down on her socializing quite a bit by then, wanting to meet the Sahotas on a regular basis reflected on the camaraderie that they had worked up over lunch.

Mike who met the Sahotas only around 2001 concurs. "Both of them have a great sense of humor," he says about Harvinder and Asha Sahota. We talk on a whole range of subjects, from politics to global affairs. He follows news quite closely on several channels, so we exchange plenty of views over there. Besides, he's my cardiologist, so I have good reason to chat on another front as well," Mike, a scientist who designs robots, says. He also talks about his internet on an amplifier that can tune into any radio anywhere in the world. It implies that through his system Mike can pick a radio station in whichever country or city that he wants, at will, and tune in. Sahota has benefited from it and says, "Yeah, he's very good. In fact, he got me Jalandhar radio station very quickly."

Over the years Nancy's managed many businesses and charities, met with numerous people from across the world, but getting to know the famous cardiologist is something she truly values. "His sense of humor, enthusiasm, and energy are probably a good match for me, because I'm high on energy as well, and not everybody is. I come away from his house thinking, 'oh what a fine guest I am'," she says, giving Sahota high marks on what a good host he is. "I usually end up telling him a funny story or two that I may not have shared with anybody else, and then he tells me all kinds of stuff," says Nancy who is presently on the Board of Trustees at the UC Berkeley Foundation. Nancy is comfortable discussing most things with Sahota, and values his opinion because "they are usually well thought out." She may not always agree with his opinions, but neither does she necessarily disagree.

For reasons that are easy to fathom Nancy has taken a liking for Indian food. While she was already introduced to spicy Indian food, the Sahotas helped them to expand on their choices. "It's fun to go to an Indian restaurant with them because we don't know how to order very well. With them around, we get interesting things we would have never picked out." She's all praise for Asha's cooking. "She's fixed a couple of nice dinners since we've been here. I am very impressed by how well she cooks," says Nancy.

ELAINE STOVEE

These days Elaine lives in an Assisted Living complex in Orange County, one she had moved in to sometime in 2014. Elaine and her husband Bob had come to occupy their house in the City of Seal Beach in Orange County in 1966. Seal Beach was an exciting place to be, it still remains the first city in Orange County right after one leaves the County of Los Angeles behind. "We could not have lived in a better city than Seal Beach," she says softly, sitting inside her compact room at the large, well-endowed complex.

Some 12 years later, Elaine and Bob watched the Sahotas move in as neighbors, and build their house. Harry was a wonderful neighbor, and a good friend of Bob's. Sahota points out, "Bob and me would have elaborate discussions on the political climate of the day. Way too much was happening and it was difficult for me to figure out who was doing what. I was new to California. So we'd sit down together, and decide whom to vote for and why," he says. In some ways Bob had become Sahota's unofficial political consultant!

It wasn't only political consultancy, though that Bob was doing. Sometimes he had to act as the security consultant of the Sahota household too! There's a small anecdote to support this. Sometime in the 1980s, Sahota, Asha, Neil and Eric were away to India on a family vacation. The keys to their house in Seal Beach were given to Elaine and Bob whom they trusted implicitly. "It is a rare thing you know," says Sahota. "You generally wouldn't trust anyone with your house keys. But Elaine and Bob were so very different." Curiously, though, the beeper in the house that was connected to Sahota's office got activated mistakenly. It had dear friend Bob totally alarmed. He had to go in to Sahota's house and check out if all was well. When the Sahotas were back, they all had a very good laugh over it.

Another incident involving Bob is etched clearly in Sahota's memory as though it took place yesterday. Bob had removed the side wheels of Eric's bicycle after checking with the little boy. But somehow Eric lost his balance, and fell hard on the road. Bob was profusely apologetic about the whole thing, even though his friend Harry kept telling him that he had done nothing wrong. "That's the kind of neighbors we were," wisecracks Elaine, raising her eyebrows.

Elaine fondly recalls the time spent with Asha, Neil and Eric. In fact, Eric was only a couple of months old, and Neil was four, when the Sahotas moved in to their Seal Beach house in 1978, so Elaine saw the boys growing up before her own eyes. By the time the Sahotas shifted to their house in Laguna Beach, Neil was 23, and Eric was just about exiting his teens.

Like Nancy, Elaine too remembers Asha, the seriously talented cook. "I'd go out in the morning, pick up my paper, and oh, there would be Asha cooking, again. I knew she just loved to cook," says Elaine. Like her, quite a few in the neighborhood would tell the Sahotas that often when they crossed their house the aroma of delicacies being prepared would waft through the air and settle down in their nostrils. This was because Asha kept the kitchen window open while cooking, and it opened out into the street. It's a habit that the former Indian Army captain has not given up and the windows remain slightly open at the Laguna Beach house too. Asha would also bring things for Elaine and Bob from her holidays, and the memories are indeed very fond.

Seeing them leave Seal Beach made Elaine sad. "When they moved to Laguna Beach, I asked them not to ever sell their house, because I didn't want anyone else in their house. I didn't want noisy neighbors. I wanted them to keep their house," says Elaine with a blissful smile spreading across her face. As if on cue Sahota adds, "And we haven't sold it, and as of now we have no plans either to do so." Elaine tells Harry to keep it forever, and he assures her that he'll do so for as long as he can. "I'm glad you advised us not to sell it, and I'm equally glad I heeded it."

Elaine was born in Long Beach, while Bob had come to California from South Dakota when he was four. They met in school, fell in love, and got married. Bob was in the Navy in the Pacific Theater of World War II, a major place of operations during the war between the Allies and Japan. "We took a lot of cruises at one time, which we thoroughly enjoyed," recalls Elaine, sitting next to a book on crosswords that helps keep her mind very sharp. "It was a little hard to get Bob started on those cruises initially, mainly because he had seen a lot of the world."

Bob passed away a month before the couple was to celebrate 64 years of married life. She lived alone at the Seal Beach house for another five years after that—in all for 48 years in that city—before selling it away and moving in to the Assisted Living complex a couple of years ago.

Truly another neighbor that the Sahotas really bond well with, and who in turn values them back. ■

FRIENDS
FOREVER

Harvinder Sahota may have been shy with fellow lady classmates at the Patiala Medical College—where for the first time in his life he studied at a co-educational institution—but over the years he became quite extroverted. His outgoing persona, his quick wit, his vast information about the world, and past and present day happenings, help him to easily mingle with people. Some of them have gone on to become fast friends. It is his numerous friendships that he cherishes the most in life.

Hubert Humphrey, a former American Vice President and a Presidential candidate, would say, "The greatest gift of life is friendship, and I've received it." Sahota, too could repeat those words, for making friends is an art that comes easily to him. Over time, his friendships have blossomed. Many go back to the time when he was in Patiala Medical College. Daya Singh Arora of Tilak Nagar, Amritsar, has known his dear friend Harvinder for 60 years. They were classmates at junior high, and then at high school. It was with Daya that Harvinder had plans to quietly slip away to Bombay and give the film world a shot. It wasn't to be, though. Daya Singh got a letter from the Life Insurance Corporation of India and did not show up at the railway station. Harvinder watched the train that was to take him to Bombay to fulfill his childhood dreams chug past him slowly and blow its sharp whistle on its way out of the platform. He was left holding a confirmed ticket. Later it dawned on him that Daya had opted for the security of a Government job in India those days over the chaotic uncertainty of the film world, and a glamour industry that was still trying to find its feet.

But one thing has remained certain—the timeless friendship that they share even now, as if it was only the other day that they were sitting in class together. Sixty years later Daya Singh says this of Harvinder: "We studied together from class one. It was clear from the very beginning that he was intelligent. He worked very hard, remained very competitive, and yet never lost the humanitarian side of his nature. You will be surprised to know that throughout school we never let any other student surpass us in academics. We were always trying to excel each other. I am all praise for who he is, and what he

(L-R) Jerry Sahota and Harjit Sahota of Vancouver, Canada, Kanwaljit Randhawa and Ajit Randhawa, Asha and Harvinder Sahota on an Alaskan Cruise

could become."

The humanitarian side to him that Daya Singh Arora talks about is evident. Dr Inder Anand has witnessed it firsthand along with the warmth of their friendship. When he was immigrating to the USA in the mid 1980s it was Sahota who helped him in that journey. Says Anand who now lives in San Diego after having worked in Minnesota for years: "He helped us get our immigration documents expeditiously by hiring an attorney with his own money. He also engaged lawyers from India to quicken the process. He is very generous with funds, and shows a genuine love for people that he helps out." It was Anand's father, Dr Santokh Singh Anand, a surgeon who became the first Director of PGIMER, Chandigarh that extended an invitation to Sahota to perform India's first angioplasty at the Institute. Inder Anand's wife, Chandana, echoes similar

LEFT: Dr Carl Clowes and his wife Dorothy who were visiting from Wales, U.K., with the Sahotas at Disneyland.
RIGHT: Dr Dhan Dev Kaushal and his wife Savita with the Sahotas inside a simulated Igloo at Hotel Monte Carlo, Las Vegas, Nevada. Dr Kaushal was the President of the Patiala Medical College alumni association and had arranged the meet in Las Vegas in 2011

sentiments. "The thing about that gentleman is how many people he's helped in addition to us. He makes it a point that nobody who comes from India goes away disappointed. It's not just about his medical contribution, he goes out of the way to help people in so many other areas. His ability to give back, and to help out is remarkable." She has more than just a word of praise for Asha as well: "Behind him is a remarkable woman who is quiet and unassuming. She, in fact, is the backbone. Dr

Sahota could not have come this far without her. There was a point when we were settling down in the West Coast when he would invite us to his home every day, and every time we arrived, she had a smile on her face. She never once grudged him for bringing us home so often. I think his success is accompanied by her ample support."

Support from Sahota is something Paul Singh, another well-wisher and friend, is familiar with. "I came to the USA about 12 years ago, and met him almost immediately after.

LEFT: With Dr Ram Kumar, Ophthalmologist from Chandigarh at the Sea World in San Diego in July 2011.
RIGHT: Bhole Brar, Dr Paul Taylor and Asha. Dr Taylor is Director, Asian Cultural History in Smithsonian Institute, Washington DC. He was involved in organizing the Sikh Artifact Exhibit at the Smithsonian and was named Paul Singh Taylor by Dr Sahota for the great interest he took in his work. His co-workers still call him Paul Singh

He is the one who gave me the opportunity to start my business. It is with his blessings that I've become who I'm. If I've been able to carve out a niche for myself, then I owe it to him. Where I'm today is because of him. There was a time when I called him four times a day, and in spite of his very busy schedule, he always was there for me. And I've seen another thing. Political leaders from Punjab make a beeline for his house, he is so popular back home too," he said in the year 2016, gratitude flowing from his voice.

Popularity and Sahota have been really good companions walking hand in hand for years. Close friend Bicky Singh of Future Solutions Inc. has seen this popularity grow over the years. He believes it is the manner in which Sahota comes forward to help people that places him above the ordinary. Says Bicky: "He's an institution in himself. I have seen him treat poor patients who do not have medical insurance. In this country, doctors won't entertain such patients, but he treats them regardless of

LEFT: Himachal Pradesh-based Dr K C Malhotra and his wife at the Sahota home in Laguna Beach in the early years of the 21st century. He studied with Harvinder Sahota at the Patiala Medical College.
RIGHT: Bahrain-based Obstetrician Dr Amarjit Kaur with the Sahotas in Artesia, Los Angeles in the early years of the 21st century. Sahota's classmate from Patiala Medical College, she delivers babies for the Royal family in Bahrain. She regularly visits her daughter in San Marino, Pasadena

LEFT: Asha and Harvinder with Swaran Kaila, wife of Anand Kaila, share a light moment outside the Kaila home in Lichfield, Staffordshire during the Sahota family visit to the U.K. in 2005. **RIGHT:** Sahota with Amrik Singh Chattha from the second batch of Patiala Medical College who was one of the founders of the alumni association. He has worked closely with Sahota to improve medical services in Patiala and other parts of Punjab, and is involved in the Smithsonian Sikh Art exhibition

whether they can pay him or not. We've also worked together at a couple of foundations internationally, and there too his generosity is in abundant display. I've known him closely also as President of the Sikh Center of Santa Ana, and he is on the Board of our Central Gurudwara."

Sahota's contribution towards Sikh heritage has received accolades from many friends. One of them is Jagjit Reyatt, an accomplished Los Angeles-based professional photographer who has done extensive work on Sikh Heritage, including coverage of three to four events in England. He has seen for himself the depths to which Harvinder Sahota has gone to catch up with Sikh history. "He is very dedicated, highly educated and extremely knowledgeable when it comes to Sikh issues. He understands the lessons of history very well, and puts them in a modern day perspective for easy understanding and reflection. And he never shies away from taking up Sikh issues which are dear to him," says Jagjit who is quite bowled over by Sahota's natural instincts to help out his community in Southern California in a mostly "gentlemanly way."

It is the quality of the work that Sahota does that makes a difference, whether helping out in the community, at the Sikh Temple, or coming to the relief of those in need, like poor patients and newcomers from India trying to establish themselves in Southern California. Harbhajan Singh Samra, called the *Okra King* of USA by *New York Times*, has known Sahota for a long time. Unhesitatingly he pronounces, "Dr Sahota never lets you down," emphasizing on *never* more than just once. He adds, "He's always there, you can count on him. He is capable of doing a lot. God has given him so much strength, so much will and so much vision that the quality of work he does becomes superior. We in the USA, therefore, have such high regard for him."

One man who's known him for a long period of time is Inder Singh, a community stalwart who has championed the

With Sir Eldon Griffiths, former MP and Minister of U.K. and Lady Betty Griffiths

Sahota with dear friend Inder Singh at home. Inder Singh is a respected Community Leader based in Tarzana, Los Angeles

LEFT: Atop a *gondola*—typically used in the Venetian canals in Italy—with Davina Changkakoti, friend from the Sahotas' days in 1974 in Rochester, New York. The picture is taken at *The Venetian* Hotel in Las Vegas, Nevada, USA.
RIGHT: Sahota with good friends Ravi Tilak (left) and Biju Patel (right), both successful businessmen and entrepreneurs

Members of the Garhdiwala Area Club assemble in Vancouver in July 2006

LEFT: Bareilly, Uttar Pradesh-based Ophthalmologist Dr Harbans Singh Dhindsa with his wife Nirmala and the Sahotas in downtown Laguna Beach. Dr Dhindsa who studied with Harvinder Sahota at Patiala Medical College has carried out thousands of cataract operations free of charge all over India. Harbans is the one who came to inform Sahota in his first year at Patiala Medical College that the students' body had unanimously elected him as its Secretary.
RIGHT: Harvinder and Asha Sahota with Dr Krishna M Reddy, Dentist

(L-R) Ajit S Randhawa, his wife Kanwaljeet, Dr Balbir Brar, his wife Bhole Brar, Harvinder and Asha Sahota come together for a picture. For 14 years, Ajit, Balbir and Harvinder regularly walked alongside one another on the beautiful sandy coastline of the Pacific at Laguna Beach

cause of the Indian diaspora not just in the West Coast and the USA, but globally as well. He says, "I've known Dr Sahota over the years to be a thorough gentleman and a highly professional and sound cardiologist. He's been a true friend, and has always been a great person to have a friendship with."

There is no doubt that Sahota has won the hearts of the larger Indian community in Southern California over and over again. Dr Jasvant Modi has seen Sahota's charitable and philanthropic side from up close, having worked with him to set up endowments and chairs at various institutions, including the University of Irvine in California. "We have worked together for many years. The thing that stands out for me is that Dr Sahota has a great heart, and is ever-willing to help other human beings. He is an asset to the entire Indian community. I know that he is well admired by his patients too, and many of those whose lives he has saved are beholden to him."

Whenever the name of the Chingkakoti couple comes up, Harvinder and Asha have a special, nostalgic look on their face. The Sahotas arrived in New York from England in the summer of 1974 in a British Airways flight that had

The Sahotas with Sir Eldon Griffiths (second from right), Muhammad Mian Soomro (center) and others at a meeting of the World Affairs Council. Soomro, incidentally, had been both President and Prime Minister of Pakistan, as well as Chairman of the Senate in his country

Asha, Gin Sidhu, wife of Anaheim Councilman Harry Sidhu, Neil (center) and Sahota (right)

(L-R) Vandana Jain, Asha, Ravi Jain, Harvinder, Sulekh Jain at the
San Diego Safari Park in February 2016. Vandana is the daughter of Ravi and Sulekh

departed London at noon. Almost immediately after, they got to know Dr Norm Chingkakoti and his ebullient wife Davina. They became such good friends that they have undertaken holiday tours together, even much after the Sahotas left New York and settled in California. Norm recalls befriending Harvinder very quickly, and remembers Neil being born before the couple's eyes. As a Supervising Physician at the program that Harvinder joined, Norm recalls Sahota's determination and drive to do well at work. "He always spoke about inventions, and worked towards them in a disciplined manner. No wonder he came up with so many patents, including the one for perfusion catheter that was a success.

(L-R) Uka Solanki, Charanjiv and her husband Joginder Singh Sidhu who in the 1980s became the inventor of the world's smallest camera, Mohinder Singh, Editor of *India Journal*, Dr Sahota, in a picture taken around the year 2000

Harvinder Sahota with friends, wine-makers, and grape-growers in Delano, San Joaquin Valley, California in the early 1990s. Fourth from right is Amar Singh Sahota, pioneer in the area who had immigrated to the USA around 1950. Third from left is Tilak Chopra who works in real estate. Second from left is Anand Kaila from England. Back at that time, Sahota and Kaila were considering buying a winery

In the front table (L-R) Dr Amarjit Singh Marwah, decorated Dentist based in Malibu, Mohinder Singh, Editor, *India Journal*, Harvinder and Asha Sahota seen on the occasion of the Patiala Medical College alumni meet organized in 1999. Dr Marwah, a doyen in dentistry, came to the USA over 60 years ago and has helped many Indians when they first arrived in Los Angeles

(L-R) Asha, Dr Kundan Singh Lidhar, Sahota's classmate during his days as a FSc student at DAV Jalandar and then again at the Patiala Medical College, Anand Kaila who was Best Man at Sahotas' wedding in U.K., Dr Jaswant Kaur Lidhar, wife of Kundan. It was a memorable evening for all at the Lidhar residence in Leeds, U.K., sometime in 2008

(L-R) Amritsar Medical College alumni Dr Sharma who loves to recite *Heer Ranjha*, the epic love story of Punjab which Sahota enjoys, Dr Satinder Dang, Dr Rani Dargan who played a key role in the organization of the Patiala Medical College alumni meet at Dana Point in 1999, Mr Paramjit Singh Dargan, Rani's husband, Sahota himself

Friends and family gather at Telford, Shropshire, U.K., during the Sahota family visit to the U.K. in 2005. Seated (from right) are Neil Sahota, Kuldip Sahota who was Labour Party MP candidate from Telford for the June 8, 2017 elections in U.K., Dr Sahota, Amrik Singh, Baldev Singh, Kundan Singh Lidhar, Surjit Singh Sahota

LEFT: Dr Sahota hosts Speaker of Punjab Assembly Dr Charanjit Singh Atwal (seated second from left) who had been Deputy Speaker of Indian Parliament, and his wife, at his Laguna Beach home.
RIGHT: At Las Vegas with Dr Narendra (Norm) Changkakoti

(L-R) Harjit Kaur Sahota, Jessi Sahota, Asha, Amrik Sahota, Jerry Sahota, Harvinder Sahota at the Garhdiwala Club celebrations in Vancouver in 2009

That was the way to go in the profession, and he led from the front."

Davina is equally gushing in her praise for Harvinder and Asha: "They are just delightful to know. Our families have remained extremely good friends. He's very good about calling, and keeping up the friendship. It's been a privilege to have known them. Dr Sahota has such an enthusiasm for knowledge, keeps up to date with developments around the world, and, of course, is a smart and brilliant doctor who has his feet firmly on the ground."

Dr Pedram Mizani, a Family Medicine specialist in Irvine who's known Dr Sahota for a long time, said in an interview: "One thing he does consistently is care for everybody around him. I've never remembered a single time when he'd not gone the distance for any of his friends or people that ask him to do something. Quite brave that he made it through everything, and against all odds, and was able to contribute so much back to humanity."

Dr Jasbir Singh Mann, President, Sikh Temple, Santa Ana, is an Orthopedic Surgeon of repute and a respected community leader. He's known his good friend Harvinder Sahota for over three decades. He points out the qualities that make Sahota a cut above the rest. "He helps everybody, he understands issues, and is a great human being. No doubt he is highly intellectual and understanding of global issues, and that quest for remaining abreast

(L-R) Davina with her husband Norm Changkakoti, Dr Alex Monteiro holding Neil who was a few months old, Monteiro's wife holding the couple's daughter about the same age as Neil, and Asha in Rochester, New York in 1975. Baby Neil looks at Davina, his Godmother, quizzically

Asha with friend Dr Srihari, a Registrar at the Maelor General Hospital at Wrexham, North Wales, in 1973

with the latest developments reflects in his profession too where he has done so much research in cardiology."

When Arun Rajaram, a Wealth Manager with Merrill Lynch, and his team at TiE invited Dr Sahota to give a lecture on entrepreneurship in the medical world sometime in November 2015 at San Diego, they were not prepared for the candidness with which the renowned cardiologist would put across his views. The audience was also struck by his humility. Sahota mentioned that making inventions was great, but one could not set aside basic bread and butter issues. "The bio-dynamics of whether things would work out or not were still uncertain when Dr Sahota started making his inventions. So he focused on practical issues, on how to feed his family first. He was not keen on projecting himself as this superstar doctor who had made no mistakes in life, and was successful from day one. He came across as a very real life hero, who mentioned why risk-taking isn't everyone's game. For such a celebrated man to put things this way before the audience was humbling," says Arun.

Pardaman Singh Sawhney from the very first batch that passed out from IIT Bombay in 1962 is a Rotarian with Newport Irvine Rotary Club. The Club invites distinguished people to give a talk on a subject of common interest on Thursdays, and one such occasion was addressed by Harvinder Sahota. "Everyone was impressed with his presentation on the future of angioplasty, the discoveries he'd made, and his patents. The important thing is that he came across as a person very keen to keep up with developments in the field, something not everyone is willing to do," says Sawhney.

Harvinder Sahota's associations inevitably go back a long way and have stood the test of time. One such association is with Bahrain-based Obstetrician Dr Amarjeet Kaur Sandhu. She is a classmate of Sahota from the Patiala Medical College, and over the years has helped deliver babies for the Royals in Bahrain. Amarjeet and her husband Manjit Singh Sandhu were looking for a match for their daughter Mita. One of the families they were talking to around the winter months of 1999 was based in Los Angeles, so the Sahotas acted as *Mama* and *Mami* on behalf of Mita and took the boy and his parents out to an Italian restaurant. Meeting over, the boy asked what should be his next step to which Sahota advised that he should fly down to Bahrain and meet the girl and her family. Eventually the two got married, thanks to the pivotal role played by the Sahotas. Mita lives in Pasadena, and Amarjeet regularly visits her daughter. Incidentally, Manjit Singh was a student of Asha's father, Mr Claire, during his days as an engineering student in India. This fact came to light much after the Sandhus had married!

A big influence in Sahota's life was Sir Eldon Griffiths, a British Conservative politician and journalist who passed away in June 2014. Sir Eldon spent half the year in warm California, and another half in England. He and Sahota, whom Sir Eldon found to be extremely inquisitive about the world around him and beyond, became thick friends. The elderly statesman that he was, Sir Eldon would talk on a range of world issues. A regular visitor to the Laguna Beach house, he would present Sahota with a number of books too, each one of them highly thought-provoking. One of the insightful discussions that Sahota had with Sir Eldon was on the British thought process before they freed India from the fetters of colonialism. Sahota says he owes a lot to the Englishman and his wife Lady Betty Griffiths for being intellectual friends and guides.

In the end, Sahota's friendships have always left a lasting impact on the lives of so many that he has touched with his irrepressible warmth and camaraderie. "My best friend is the one who brings out the best in me," Henry Ford, founder of the Ford Motor Company, would say. Sahota's friends echo similar sentiments as well. ∎

Sahotas with Nicole Balsamo,
Executive Director of
Advancement School of
Humanities at the UCI

CHAIRS, CHARITIES AND UNIVERSITIES

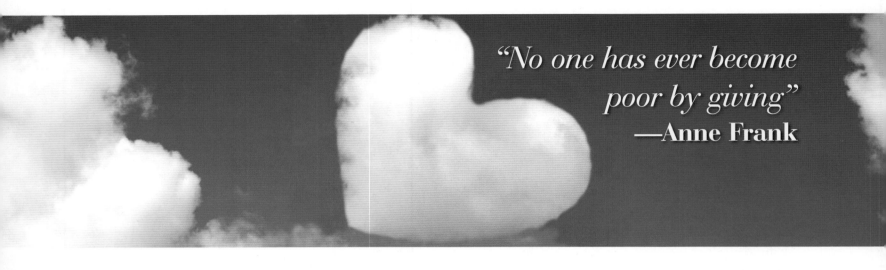

"No one has ever become poor by giving"
—**Anne Frank**

Harvinder Sahota's generous and philanthropic side comes out very prominently in his contributions towards academics in the Southern California area. The most significant contribution was made in 2015 when he established, in the name of his mother, the Bibi Dhan Kaur Sahota Chair for Studies in Sikh Religion at the School of Humanities at the University of California at Irvine (UCI). His mother who prayed for him fervently when he had been declared dead as a fourteen-day-old infant in 1941, and someone who instilled in him deep moral values in life, has always remained close to Harvinder Sahota's heart. To set up the Chair, he made an endowment of USD 1.5 million to UCI's Department of Humanities.

Mother Bibi Dhan Kaur Sahota

The UCI itself was founded in 1965 and today is one of the most dynamic campuses in the USA. It happens to be the second-largest employer in Orange County. The New York Times named UCI as number one among U.S. universities that do the most for low-income students. It is one of 62 universities in the U.S. and Canada that has been elected to membership of the prestigious Association of American Universities. In terms of annual economic impact, the UCI generates USD 5 billion.

Harvinder Sahota points out that the process is on to select a tenured professor for the chair established in the name of his mother, and that it will be a permanent position. All aspects of Sikh Religion will be taught, most likely from the start of the 2017 fall semester. The salaries of professors will be met till perpetuity. Sahota's endowment amount will be bolstered by additional funds from the UCI which will help fund student activities and administrative expenses.

Professor Georges Van Den Abbeele, Dean, School of Humanities, UCI, has this to say about the Bibi Dhan Kaur Sahota Chair: "I think the step taken by Dr Harvinder Sahota is a very important one. Sikhs are a large and very significant community worldwide. In the USA they have been severely misunderstood, at times, even though their contribution historically is immense. The courses will be worked out by faculty members. They will teach Sikhism from the point of view of other religions like Christianity, Islam, Judaism and Jainism."

The School of Humanities is the largest one in the UCI in terms of faculty. There are 13 departments that offer thousands of courses in subjects such as Philosophy, History, English, European Languages, East Asian and Asian Languages, Spanish, Afro-American Studies, Asian American Studies, Media and a lot more. Dean Abbeele puts it succinctly when he says, "Humanities also prepares you for all the other things that happen to us in life, things that truly matter, such as love, beauty, the challenges of leadership, the richness of human

Asha, Sahota and Abbeele signing the agreement for the USD 1.5 million endowment at University of California at Irvine

Sahota with Dean Abbeele who is wearing a beautiful turban at his office at UCI

Dean William Maurer from the School of Social Sciences at UCI with Dr Sahota and Dean Abbeele in February 2017

experience, the courage to think for oneself and the ability to follow those paths less travelled."

Abbeele is all praise for Sahota for having set up the Chair. "It has been a wonderful honor to work with Dr Sahota who is a most generous and intelligent man. He has offered us good advice, and provided good feedback. Somewhere he is extremely loyal, open and frank. I have enormous respect for him and am always happy to see him."

The Sahotas' association with UC Irvine does not end with the Chair, though. Elder son Neil studied at the UCI. In fact even as a child he desired to attend this University, and didn't want to look beyond, unlike younger brother Eric who explored the East Coast of the USA for higher studies and eventually joined the Johns Hopkins University in Baltimore. Today, Neil is an Adjunct Professor at UCI's Merage School of Business, and lives on campus. He happens to be an IBM Master Inventor and a World Wide Business Development Leader in the IBM Watson Group, working with a wide range of global clients to ideate next

LEFT: Sahotas with Goran Matjiasevic, Senior Assistant Vice Chancellor, UCI (left) and Diane Lamperts, Director, Chancellor Club, UCI (in green) during the Chancellor Club reception held on the occasion of the New Swan Shakespeare Festival on August 5, 2016. **RIGHT:** The annual Sikh-Jain function in Loyola Marymount University, Los Angeles. Sitting on ground is Professor Nirinjan Kaur Khalsa, an American Sikh (second from right). In the back row are Dr Sahota (fourth from left), Professor Chris Chapple (third from right), Dr Arvind Pal Singh Mandair (second from right) from the University of Michigan, Sulekh Jain (fourth from right). The image in the background shows *Takhat Patna Sahib*, birthplace of Guru Gobind Singh Ji, Tenth Sikh Guru, and to the right is the Old Jain Temple. Guru Ji was born here in a Jain family home that later donated land where the *Takhat* stands

generation products and solutions.

One person who's known Sahota for over five years is Houston-based Dr Sulekh Jain who has helped set up along with Dr Nitin Shah a Chair on Jain Studies at the UCI. The funding for the Jain Studies came mainly from Dr Jaswant Modi, the Jain community and Manu Shah who combined to put up an endowment totaling USD 1.5 million.

Jain calls Sahota his "soul brother" and adds with a dash of humor that when they meet, they refer to each other as Harvinder *Jain* and Sulekh *Sahota*. Together they discussed the setting up of the chairs at the UCI. Jain puts matters in perspective, "Jains and Sikhs have co-existed for 500 years.

Jain *sadhus* have also come from Sikh traditions. When Jains have travelled on foot, they've very often stayed with Sikh families. Our communities go back a long way."

In 2012, together they set up courses for teaching Sikh and Jain faiths at the Claremont School of Theology (CST) and Claremont Lincoln University (CLU), two institutions where Sahota has served as a board member. While the inception of CST goes back to the late 19th century, the CLU was established in 2011 and is an accredited online graduate university that offers, among others, a master's degree in Interfaith Action.

At the same time they also created a Center for Sikh

LEFT: Sahotas with friends Maya Matkin (left), Gary Matkin, Rekha Joshi and Jeanne Leitner (fourth, fifth and sixth from left) outside an open-air amphitheater at the UCI styled along the lines of Globe Theatre in U.K. Here the Chancellor's Club had hosted the *Hamlet* by UCI students in August 2016. **RIGHT:** Dr Sahota with Zak Houston who gave a brilliant rendition of the lead character *Hamlet* in the eponymous Shakespearian play

and Jain Studies at the nearly 100-year-old Loyola Marymount University (LMU) that follows Jesuit and Marymount traditions.

Here they have a fulltime three-year tenure professor, Nirinjan Kaur Khalsa, an American Sikh. She has been hired from the University of Michigan at Ann Arbor to teach both courses. The funding commitment, as of now, is for three years. Efforts, though, are on to make it a permanent position. Most of the funding for the Sikh Chairs has, of course, come from the cardiologist with a generous heart, Harvinder Sahota.

Similar semester for both Sikh and Jain studies have been set up at the San Diego State University, the third oldest university in the 23-member California State University system that has more than 35,000 students and an alumni base of 280,000. Likewise, talks are on with the University of California at Merced—the newest campus within the UC System—as well. Typically, after the funding has been committed and accepted by the academic institution, it takes about a year to put the processes in place, identify the instructor, and have the course running. The most laudable part is that the courses in Sikh Studies which are being sponsored by Sahota are in some of the most reputed institutions in California.

He also has plans to extend his endowments to create Sikh study programs in discussions with academic

Sahota at the UCI Alumni Building where his name (circled) along with
Asha's figures prominently in the list of generous donors. Neil's name is to the right

institutions in Richmond in Virginia, Denver in Colorado, Princeton in New Jersey and Houston in Texas. The average enrollment at these courses is about 30 each semester at the undergraduate level. Once interests in Sikh Studies heighten, students can join Master and PhD programs.

Sahota's connection with the Jain community in California happened by chance after he met Sulekh Jain. But he soon realized that his connect with the community

Speaking at the Smithsonian Institution where he had made a sizeable contribution to an exhibition on Sikhs

goes back a long way. His elder brother did a BA in Math from the D.C. Jain College in Ferozepur Cantonment.

Another leading light of the Jain community in the USA is anesthesiologist Dr Nitin Shah who helps run surgical camps in the USA, Africa and India along with Sulekh Jain. He says that the Jains were the first to start a course at the CST in September 2011. Later on, the Sikh courses were added by Dr Sahota. He is all praise for the contribution to UCI made by the Sahotas and says: "It is a phenomenal thing that Dr Sahota and his wife have done to benefit undergraduate students who want to study Sikhism at a mainstream American university. He is a wonderful, down-to-earth individual, who indeed does what he commits."

Sahota has contributed and sponsored generously to the UCI, CLU, CST, LMU, San Diego State University, and the school and college that he attended back in Punjab. He's invested in being a life member of the prestigious Chancellor Club at the UCI where donations range between USD 25,000 to USD 50,000. The Club utilizes these funds to help pay for tuition and books for deserving students, explores job opportunities for those passing out. Also, Sahota and his elder son Neil have each contributed separately to the UCI's Alumni Building. The contribution by the two of them has been about USD 100,000.

It is well known that in the USA those running for political offices like President, Governor, Congress and the Senate get huge contributions from individuals, and firms across sectors like finance, oil, banking, insurance, pharmaceuticals, devices and equipment, arms, defense and many more. As an individual, in his own generous way, Sahota has always helped out those running for different offices.

Dr Sohan Singh Chaudhury from Pittsburgh who came to the USA in 1960 to join a PhD program in Chemistry at the University of California in Davis has known Sahota for a long time, and has been witness, first hand, to his charitable nature. He says, "Dr Sahota has donated money very generously and supported many projects in the USA. When we had a Sikh exhibit at the Smithsonian, he was one of the top supporters, both in terms of funds, and time and energy. When a friend went to his house to collect money for the Sikh Gallery, he immediately cut the very first donation check for USD 10,000. Later he added more money, taking the total to USD 50,000."

They say no one has become poor from giving. One thing is for sure. Sahota's soul is infinitely richer from his acts of philanthropy. ∎

OPINIONS AND VIEWS ON WORLD AFFAIRS

World views cannot be shaped in a day. You need to ponder and reflect for hours, weeks, and months. You need to read up, listen, and watch, very carefully. You need to pause, and reflect, again and again. You must think beyond the obvious and the immediate, connect with the Universe, and only then will the deeper, hidden messages of life get conveyed to you.

Watchful thinking will make you intuitive, and develop inside you the ability to grasp that which is not visible to the naked eye. In the intangibles lie life's greatest truths. World views of the higher kinds cannot simply be shaped in a day. And so it has been the case with Dr Harvinder Sahota, cardiologist, philanthropist, parent, husband, friend, well-wisher, and so much more, whose world views have taken time to form.

Sahota's pondered and reflected quite a bit in life, and on life itself. He is an avid follower of television channels that dwell into history and go well behind the scenes to probe hard and dig deep. He culls out information from several different places, and does not depend on any single source. He believes in the power of the printed word, and his understanding is that it is the most reliable. It is in the details that value addition takes place, and printed newspapers provide those along with better background information and analyses. In comparison, information on television and radio is by-and-large fleeting, constantly changing, and lacking in depth. Breaking news on TV and internet comes and goes too fast. The printed word in newspapers and magazines stays.

The cardiologist has an innate ability to intellectually engage on a subject that he thinks is of relevance. He is a practical, generous man who sometimes deliberately allows his heart to rule his mind. His views are worth listening to. Sahota has seen quite a bit of life, and his views would have evolved over the years through his education, his numerous fellowships, his travels, his attempts at business, his inventions, his charity and community work. He is an eyewitness to a fair amount of world history.

He has learnt that life is constantly evolving. No man, after all, steps in the same river twice, for it is not the same river, neither is he the same man.

He has firm opinions and views on several subjects.

Sahota in his living room immersed in thoughts

Let's look at some of them:

HEALTH CARE IN THE USA

Health care, no doubt, has remained a big issue in the USA. Sahota feels it has not been addressed with the degree of scientific attention and precision that the subject verily demands. Even after so many years, the USA has not been able to strike at the root of the health care delivery problem.

The irony in large measure is that those who are drafting the nation's health plans, and crafting the rules and regulations for health care for its over 321 million people, are not the ones that have worked as medical doctors in small towns and cities where most of the US population lives. They have little or no hands-on knowledge about what doctors and patients go through in small and mid-sized towns on a daily basis. Qualified and experienced people that have worked in countries like Canada and Britain for some years are not a part of the decision-making process for drawing up health plans. "Overall, it means that political appointees with no experience in working in small towns, ones that are largely unqualified without proper knowledge, are making the decisions in health care and calling the shots. This is not good for America's health," says Sahota with the kind of frankness that we'd expect of him. As a result there is a mismatch between public expectation and actual delivery on the ground. It leaves the final health care system vulnerable and open to constant scrutiny and unwanted criticism.

The advisors on Health Care committees are recommended and appointed by politicians whose pool of contacts is quite limited. The appointees try eagerly to remain politically correct and are recommending what their bosses want to hear and not what the masses want, according to Sahota. There is a good chance, he says, that those who drafted Obamacare are themselves unclear about its content. The same goes for Members of Congress and Senators. "This can be corrected by selecting and involving the right kind of people to improve America's health care system," the heart doctor says.

In Sahota's opinion, the best health care system that he has seen working like a well-lubricated machine from close quarters is the one in Britain. Prime Minister Margaret Thatcher said there would be NHS for everybody and additionally there would be private insurance for those who wanted to buy it separately. Quite rightly, Sahota calls it the Hybrid System. "Clearly NHS has worked wonderfully since 1948. Otherwise health services would have been an election issue, and the British would have changed it within one election cycle," says Sahota.

Within the ambit of overall health care, there is another significant issue that has been on Sahota's mind for the last 15-20 years. In fact, he posted letters on the subject to the top national medical colleges in India (All India Institute of Medical Science, New Delhi), Pakistan (Lahore and Karachi), Bangladesh (Dhaka), and to medical colleges in Punjab (Chandigarh, Patiala, Faridkot). It relates to Normal Value for medical parameters in case of Europeans on the one hand, and Asians and Africans on the other. He points out that it is a fact that the body structure (height, weight, bone formation) and genetics of the Caucasian population is different from that of the Asian population. But the current system of trials, experiments, dosages for drugs is worked on the basis of European population, and not the Asian population. He, in fact, is yet to see a single study where Normal Value has been established on Asians. Sahota firmly believes that Normal Values should be calculated independently for all Asians, as well as for all other races.

An Asian management system for body chemistry, drugs dosages and trials needs to be worked out. "Europeans have different blood count levels, calcium and potassium levels, blood pressure and so on. These parameters are different for African and Asian races. Asians

ABOVE: A smile to go with the brilliant flowers.
RIGHT: Tomatoes from the garden, and in the background a banana tree

Sahota has a wonderful garden at Laguna Beach and enjoys watering the plants

should have their own medical studies and trials in their own countries, and report the findings in their own medical journals and books rather than depending on Western studies," says Sahota, keen that the current lop-sided situation is rectified at the earliest possible.

EUTHANASIA

"In one of the hospitals, I as a Member of the Ethics Departmental Committee was discussing this subject. Some of the doctors were in favor of euthanasia but I was firmly against it. I said that I'd become a doctor to save lives, to prolong lives, and not to take lives. I cannot be instrumental in killing a human being. Also, I said that we may not have a cure for certain diseases today, but you never know, there may be a breakthrough tomorrow. I've given instructions to my family that they should never say yes to pulling the plugs off," says Sahota.

"Many patients have recovered after years in coma. There is a host of medication available today to alleviate pain, and suffering. Those should be provided to give relief, instead of opting for euthanasia," he says.

DOWRY

Sahota learnt about the dowry system early in life and knew straightaway that it was an abhorrent custom where the daughter had to be literally "sold" to the groom's family. Growing up, he was appalled by the undue emphasis placed on dowry—amount of property or money brought by a bride to her husband as part of an unwritten marriage settlement.

"It is a disgusting practice. Once it starts, it becomes never ending. Each time the woman returns from her parent's house, she is expected to bring back something substantial. When a child is born, the boy's side expects more dowry. The girl's life becomes miserable, she is tortured for dowry. Sometimes we have learnt that the girl was set on fire by the in-laws, even though it was passed off as an accident. It results in complete breakdown of marital peace," explains Sahota.

THE INDIAN CONUNDRUM

Sahota has been hearing Indian leaders talking very highly about India for a very long time. If one were to believe each and every word of such political people, then by now India should have been the next big Monaco. Even Indian newspapers in the USA are quite busy singing praises about India—about the country's huge cellular phone market, its growing number of car owners who can afford new and pre-owned vehicles at low prices and small loans, the burgeoning fast food chains with their hamburgers and French fries, and so on. But the point to be noted is that India is another Loan Economy. "According to me it is still a superficial economy and all this talk about India becoming rich is misunderstood. When people are in debt, everything they possess becomes a façade. India's vast young population, in particular, is borrowing a lot and does not have solid money," says Sahota.

An Indian journalist once told him that if a newspaper started writing real stories on India, no one would buy the newspapers, and hardly anyone would advertise. "Dr Sahota, these newspapers cannot afford to be critical of India. Indians in the USA and in India want to hear positive things on India. As a business, it is important for us to give our readers what they want," the journalist told Sahota. The cardiologist feels that the job of the media is to provide facts. "Let the judgment be left to readers," he says.

Sahota is quick to spot the Paradox. Every week hundreds of Indians queue up outside the Consulates and the Embassy of the USA in India, and the High Commissions of Canada, Australia, U.K. and New Zealand, wanting to emigrate. They include doctors, IT engineers, politicians, movie stars. If

Watering the Manila Mango tree and talking about the mangoes at the kitchen table

LEFT: Sir Eldon Griffiths speaks at the American Heart Association Award ceremony where Sahota was honored. **RIGHT:** With Sandy, daughter of Sahota's sister, at home in Laguna Beach. Sandy grew up in Kenya before her parents emigrated to the USA

India's situation was truly so inviting, then the reverse should have been true. Then there should have been big lines of Americans outside Indian consulates queuing up to emigrate to India. "I don't think the rhetoric of Indian leaders and the media quite matches up with the reality on the ground," says Sahota. "I will only believe the India story of progress when emigration to the West goes down and Indians in America start packing up and return to India voluntarily. And also I'd like to see local Americans emigrating to India," he adds.

DEMOCRACY

When it comes to the word *democracy*, it is different strokes for different folks. Almost anyone who has anything to do with the concept has his own version of the subject. Every nation differs in the way it practices its democracy. Chinese democracy is different from American democracy, which in turn is different from British democracy and Indian democracy. Sahota says that you cannot pinpoint any one form as being the real democracy, because they vary from each other across the world. "The closest that comes to being a true democracy is perhaps the one practiced in Britain," he says. "By and large, the money spent is kept to the minimum, and the elections get over quickly. They don't drag for months and years like in some other nations," says the cardiologist.

After watching democracy unfold before his eyes over so many decades around the world, Sahota, the keen student and observer, makes a few valid points. He says that when a political candidate concentrates solely on winning votes by making promises that he knows cannot be fulfilled (in case he wins), panders indiscriminately to vote banks, flexes his financial muscle, it simply becomes a recipe for getting a poor democracy. Also, many right-thinking people stay away, because for them getting into politics is like stepping into murky waters. "As long as the best do not get into politics, can you call it real democracy?" Sahota asks. "Does it not become less than good democracy?"

Millions and billions of dollars are raised for a single position in the USA every four years. The bitter campaigns that pretty much get extremely personal towards the end go on for years. Lobbyists get heavily involved. "In the long run one must find a way out of this needless expenditure done in the name of political donations and support. It is wasteful, and can be used for other humanitarian purposes," Sahota states. There is way too much dependence on TV ratings and opinion polls. Whether they are real, or propped up, is anybody's guess. The constitutional founders may not have conceived it that way, especially at a time over 200 years ago when there was no television to run elections, no internet to conduct online polls, and influence voters through text and electronic mail.

Also, what has been seen over the years in the USA is that several former Presidents, Senators, and Members of Congress have turned into lobbyists and consultants, and end up charging exorbitant amounts of money for their services. Some even get hundreds of thousands of dollars for simply delivering speeches. When money becomes the central goal of political activity, democracy loses a bit of its sheen, and principles, says the cardiologist.

MISSED OPPORTUNITIES

Sahota had just arrived in England when John Enoch Powell, the sitting MP from Wolverhampton South West, delivered a controversial speech in April 1968. In his *Rivers of Blood* speech, Powell who had served as Minister of Health in Prime Minister Harold Macmillan's cabinet in the early 1960s, strongly criticized Commonwealth immigration to the U.K. He had mentioned that if immigration from India and Pakistan went unchecked, rivers of blood would flow in the streets of London and other British cities.

LEFT: Pointing at the roses in the front driveway with the Pacific Ocean in the horizon.
RIGHT: Feeding the birds is part of Dr Sahota's daily routine. And, amazingly, the birds use their internal clock to fly in to his garden in the morning and in the afternoon to nibble at the feed

LEFT: Showing the eggplant growth. **RIGHT:** A delightful mix of flowers in the garden area always help in adding to the thought process

Sahota says that while Powell had thrown political correctness to the winds, Britain perhaps had missed an opportunity to tighten its immigration laws—a subject of raging debate in the nation nearly five decades later.

Likewise, an opportunity, says Sahota, was missed by not enforcing the Rajiv-Longowal Accord in the Punjab of the 1980s. "Political correctness is something which ignores the common good of the masses. The reverberations of an opportunity missed will be felt long after it has come and gone," says Sahota. Powerful words, well delivered.

Sahota also recalls a discussion he had with former Saudi Ambassador Prince Turki Al Faisal in November 3, 2016 in Orange County. He asked him why there was no European Union-style organization in the Middle East. The ambassador bluntly told the cardiologist that the idea had been discussed but had failed to take off. Sahota also asked the Saudi diplomat why a NATO-like alliance could not be forged in the Middle East to which the response was that the concerned countries could not be brought together in agreement, which, of course, was a mistake.

DISCRIMINATION, ILLEGALITY AND INDIAN IMMIGRANTS

There is always this comparison game, and questions come up on how fairly Indians get treated in the U.K. and in the USA. Are Indians more discriminated against in England, and less so in the USA? Sahota who emigrated from India and worked in England for seven years (1967-1974) before migrating for the second time in his life to the USA in 1974, has analyzed this oft-repeated question.

His response is typical of a man who is keen to get straight into the heart of the matter. Indians who were working in British colonies in Africa had a choice to leave and go to the U.K. in the 1960s, or return to India. Almost all chose the U.K. over India. Also few Indians were emigrating to the USA at that time because laws for Indian immigration were rather strict. He has found that discrimination has been there in England, it is there in the USA. Only time frames are different. "When I went to England there was no shortage of labor. Jobs for doctors and engineers had already been taken. So it wasn't easy getting jobs. Naturally some amount of discrimination crept in, and local British people were preferred over migrating Indians. The situation was much more acute in semi-skilled areas," the cardiologist says. "The situation for Indian immigrants to the U.K. in the 1960s should be compared to Indian immigrants to the USA in the 1990s and early 21st century. By comparing apples with apples, one can put things in perspective," Sahota adds.

When in 1967 Sahota arrived for the first time in England, he kept enough money aside to buy a one-way ticket back to India. He'd told himself that if at any point in time he found the British environment not conducive and not up to his expectations, he'd return. "If my stay in England had turned sour, if I'd felt insulted at any point, if I were to be mistreated, if I couldn't find work even after being a doctor, or if circumstances forced me to do a job at a place I did not like, I would not have stayed back in England," he says, looking back at the years that have rolled by. He says although there were several people even back in the 1960s in India who'd give an arm and a leg to somehow get to Britain, he was intensely determined not to ever be a part of that motley, migratory crowd.

Before he made up his mind to move to England, he was clear about the things he wouldn't do at any cost—he would not produce any false certificates, lie about his background in order to get a visa or a job, or devise any other illegality to get there. For Sahota, the same thought process applied in the USA. He always had money set aside for a one-way ticket to India. In fact, in 1980 when his elder sister and her family came on a visitor's visa to the USA and decided not to return, Sahota would have nothing of it. He politely but firmly asked her to return to India, join the emigration queue and then come back with proper documents if she wanted to stay in the USA. Eventually, she made it to the US in 1989.

It saddens him to see the desperation that has crept in among many Indians to leave India at any cost. "Look what's going on today," he says in an anguished tone. "It is documented that a large number of Indians in the USA are illegal. Homeland Security data show 30,000 Indians overstayed in the USA in 2016 alone. Over the years 600,000 Indians have crossed the porous Mexican border without valid documents. There are those who arrive in the USA on a visitor's visa, and then simply vanish. Several students who came to the USA to complete their studies never did so, instead they started working illegally," he says, piqued at the embarrassment caused to the larger Indian community by this kind of unlawful and desperate behavior.

"There are Indians in the USA who are supposed to declare their total annual income every year, including that from India—things like pension drawn, if any, income from businesses, interest on bank deposits in India, income from property or agriculture. Many times such incomes are never disclosed. These people meet the definition of being illegal quite accurately," the cardiologist says, once again mincing no words.

If he wasn't accepted in the U.K. rightfully, Sahota says he was quite prepared to return to India and stick it out. He was prepared to put on the traditional *kurta* and pyjama, get a stethoscope around his neck, and start seeing patients in his hometown, Garhdiwala, whether he earned enough or not. "I was not much sold on any country. But the turning point that decided for me that I was going to settle in the West was when my first child, Neil, was born in New York in 1974. Later Eric was born in California in 1978,"

he says. By then he was keen to settle down after being on the road for 14 years doing fellowships in England, USA and Canada, since earning his MBBS degree from the Patiala Medical College.

On discrimination, he has another view. Indians in the IT sector in the USA have resigned themselves to the fact that they would be paid less than par wages. "If they were to demand the same minimum pay that needs to be paid to their American counterparts, there would be fewer openings for them," Sahota points out. He cites a few examples in Southern California to buttress his argument. The Walt Disney Company and the Southern California Edison brought IT engineers from India. They asked the local American staff to train and supervise them. When the training was over, they retained the Indians at much lower pay, and pink-slipped many of the local staff. In Sahota's judgment this amounts to "high class discrimination." Somewhat similar is the situation in the California University as well. "My question is simple," says Sahota. "If Indians on H-1B visas start demanding equal pay and working conditions, how many will continue to retain their jobs?" For sure, it wouldn't take a rocket scientist to answer this one!

SIR ELDON GRIFFITHS

Sir Eldon Griffiths had won a by-election from a constituency in Suffolk County in 1964 and represented the seat until his retirement in 1992. He had also served as a Junior Minister for Environment and Sport in the British Government for four years in the 1970s. Sahota and he had a great relationship going. It was he who arranged for Sahota to be Chief Guest at a function at the Cambridge University where a dinner was thrown in honor of the cardiologist and his wife Asha by the President. Sahota was taken around the hospital and its medical wing. Sir Eldon also arranged for the Sahotas to visit Suffolk County. Says

Sahota: "He was very good with me. And we were also very good to him. He would introduce me to many people, and each time asked me for a copy of my first biography that he could hand over to people as an introduction."

Sir Eldon called Sahota a global citizen. He also saw in him an intelligent, kind and a nice man, a friend, and above all a person with a panoramic view of the world. In an interview, Sir Eldon says, "The first thing to me about Harvinder Sahota is that he's not just a surgeon, he's not just a doctor, he's a great human being and is very kind. He and his wife are among the kindest people I've known. And the second thing about him is his inquisitiveness, he really wants to know. He is a global citizen. He comes from the Punjab. He was educated in part in England and in Wales. Then he came to the US and particularly to California. This has made him in every sense an international person. He's a very good friend to have."

The Elveden Estate, near London, houses the Palace of Maharaja Duleep Singh, the last ruler in the Sikh Empire. It also has a life-size statue of Duleep Singh, and everyone recalls the "Maharaja" easily. It happened to be in Sir Eldon's constituency. Duleep Singh is buried there alongside his wife and children. Even though Sikhs have offered to buy the Palace, its current owner has declined all offers. It was Duleep Singh who gave the *Koh-i-Noor*, the largest diamond, to Queen Victoria under circumstances that are yet unclear. At the palace, Sahota met Navtej Singh Sarna who was releasing his book *The Exile* on Duleep Singh. Sahota received a signed copy of the book from Sarna, an outstanding diplomat who has served as India's Ambassador to Israel (2008-2012) and was appointed India's Ambassador to the USA in September 2016. Earlier, in January 2016, he had taken charge as Indian High Commissioner to the U.K. He also happened to be the longest-serving spokesperson of India's Foreign Ministry. In 2008, when a few Sikhs met with Charles, Prince of Wales, at

the St James's Palace, one of them, Colonel Harinder Singh Attari, a retired Indian Army officer, claimed that the *Koh-i-Noor* belonged to his family. He went on to explain to Charles that he was the great-grandson of General Sham Singh Attariwala (in whose memory Colonel Attari's building a museum in Attari, Punjab), one of the top generals of Maharaja Ranjit Singh (father of Maharaja Duleep Singh) to whose family Colonel Attari's wife belonged. There was, though, absolutely no response or reaction from Charles to this piece of important revelation by Attari. Sahota was privy to this piece of history-unfolding conversation, or, should we just say, the lack of it.

SIKHS

Dr Sahota's own interests in the Sikh community and his contributions have not gone unnoticed by his American friends. Soon after Sahota set up the Dhan Kaur Sahota Presidential Chair in Sikh Studies at the University of California at Irvine in December 2015, one of his good friends, Congressman Edward R Royce wrote: "Today, UCI, with the strong support of the Sahotas, has taken a leadership role by designing programs to educate anyone interested in Sikh culture, heritage and the Punjabi language…I would like to thank Drs Harvinder and Asha Sahota for their dedication and personal contributions to society. Would especially like to commend Dr Harvinder Sahota for his unwavering commitment to the betterment of society—from pioneering lifesaving angioplasty techniques to his continued contributions to educational opportunities he is a great representative of the Sikh community." (See earlier chapter on *Chairs, Charities and Universities*).

Indeed, Sahota has taken a leadership role in affairs of the Sikh community in the USA. He was part of the 50th Anniversary Program of the Sikh Foundation in San Francisco in May 2017 where he met Canadian Minister for

LEFT: Sahota at Stanford University with Montek Singh Ahluwalia, former Deputy Chairman of the Planning Commission and his wife Ishwer Judge Ahluwalia, Chairperson, Board of Governors, Indian Council for Research on International Economic Relations. **RIGHT:** Sahota with Dennis Ross, a diplomat heavily involved in the Israeli-Palestinian peace process during the Bush and Clinton administrations

LEFT: The Sahotas with Chancellor of the University of California, Irvine, Howard Gillman, in May 2017. **RIGHT:** Dr Sahota seen with Alejandra Garcia Williams, a former Counselor of Mexico in California. She appreciated the fact that the cardiologist introduced Angioplasty procedure in Guadalajara, Mexico

National Defence Harjit Singh Sajjan. Minister Sajjan who is an MP from Vancouver South was also recently on an official trip to India where he was well received by the Modi Government. In San Francisco, Sahota also met Dr Anarkali Kaur Honaryar, an ex-senator and prominent Sikh Afghan politician, and a dentist. He took her to be introduced to Sajjan, himself a combat veteran who as a member of the Canadian Armed Forces undertook three tours to Afghanistan. Later that day, Sajjan gave away an award to Honaryar.

Sajjan happens to be the only turbaned Sikh cabinet minister in the world. As Minister for National Defence in Canada, he works closely with the US Secretary of Defense. He is one of four Sikh ministers in Canada. The others are Infrastructure Minister Amarjeet Sohi, Small Business Minister Bardish Chagger and Innovation Minister Navdeep Singh Bains. In fact at an interaction with students of the American University in Washington DC, Canadian Prime Minister Justin Trudeau had wittily quipped in March 2017 that his cabinet had more Sikh ministers than that of the BJP-led Modi Government in India. There are also 17 Sikh MPs in Canada—16 from the Liberal Party and one from the Conservative Party. In contrast, there are two women Sikh Federal Ministers in India, Maneka Gandhi and Harsimrat Kaur Badal.

The cardiologist says that it gladdened his heart to find so many prominent Sikhs that have made the community proud at the San Francisco gathering. These people occupy eminent positions in several countries across the world and in all walks including holding public office, and being a part of administration, law and order, armed forces, medicine, law, media, architecture, engineering, real estate, farming, business, to name a few. In his own country, USA, Sahota singles out Nikki Haley for her exceptional rise. Governor of South Carolina between January 2011 and January 2017, Haley, born

Canadian Minister for National Defence Harjit Singh Sajjan presents an award to Dr Anarkali Kaur Honaryar, ex-senator and prominent Sikh Afghan politician, at a Sikh Foundation program in San Francisco in May 2017

Nimrata Randhawa, is the current US Ambassador to the UN. Overall, Sahota says the contribution of Sikhs to the USA is immense, especially in areas of space, science, medicine, engineering, business, politics, and more recently in the US Army, and law and order.

Sahota points out that the demographics of the Indian population in the USA are different from the Indian population in India. By that he means that there are more Hindus in India than Muslims and Sikhs. In the USA and Canada, however, the demographics are totally different. Sikhs make up the largest numbers within the Indian population in these countries. He is happy to note that within the USA many attempts are being made to provide a better understanding of Sikhs, and Sikhism. Towards this end, television advertisements, displays at the Smithsonian in Washington DC, work by Sikh lawyers, are no doubt helping to give a clear picture of Sikhs. "I'm glad to see many more Sikhs today with long hair and wearing turban

LEFT: With Felix Pugrad, an Echo Tech who's been associated with Bellflower Clinic for over 35 years.
RIGHT: (L-R) Mary Roosevelt, wife of James Roosevelt, eldest son of President Franklin Delano Roosevelt and Eleanor Roosevelt, Gisela Landreville and Asha Sahota. Mary and James were instrumental in getting the Chancellor's Club at the UCI off the ground

LEFT: Madeena Rafiq, Director of Operations at World Affairs Council-Orange County (left) with Kunga Wangmo Operational Assistant. **RIGHT:** (L-R) Harry Sidhu, President Jerry Campbell, now Director and President Emeritus, Claremont Lincoln University (CLU), Provost Phillip Clayton, Sir Eldon Griffiths, Dr Sahota during the inauguration of the Sikh Center at the CLU in February 2013. The three of them were honored with turbans.
Jerry is a former President of the CLU as well as former President of Claremont School of Theology

in the USA than was the case earlier," the cardiologist says.

On the subject of Sikhism, Sahota revisits some important areas. He says that the only prohibition in the Sikh religion is the use of tobacco, and smoking. Sahota says that what science has been discovering of late was written 500 years ago in the *Guru Granth Sahib* (Sikh Holy Bible). For instance, the *Guru Granth Sahib* said there were lakhs of Universes, and today's space scientists are realizing it. He says that the concept of networking was brilliantly put in practice by the Sikh Gurus. Guru Gobind Singh Ji, the Tenth Sikh Guru, said that every Sikh man should have *Singh* (meaning lion) as his middle name, and every woman should have *Kaur* as her's. "This helped connect Sikhs all over with that link," he says. Sikhs also have their Vatican and Pope at the Golden Temple in Amritsar, as well as the Sikh Parliament—the Shiromani Gurdwara Parbandhak Committee (SGPC). When he was in conversation with the RSS leaders, Sahota pointed out that but for the sacrifice of Sikhs and the Sikh Gurus, today's India would not be a multi-religious, multi-ethnic and multi-cultural country. The RSS leaders strongly agreed with him.

MEETING WITH RSS LEADERS

Sahota says that if the Governments and politicians of the day work honestly, do what is right for the majority of the people, are not concerned too much about being re-elected but are sincerely concerned with delivering better nations, and are not too busy being politically correct, then one thing is certain: those politicians who run Governments are bound to be re-elected. But for doing all that, there needs to be firm political will, and a lack of interference from the political parties.

In May 2017, Sahota met London-based Ram Vaidya, a leading *pracharak* of the Hindu Swayamsevak Sangh (regarded as the U.K. branch of the RSS). Earlier, in 2016 he had met with V Bhaigaih who had been appointed as the 4th *Sah-Sarakaryavah* (Joint General Secretary) of the RSS' national team in March 2015. "After talking to them, I was deeply impressed by their long-term vision for India and how they have plans to take the country forward as a 21st century superpower. They said their agenda was drawn up at team meetings at the highest levels and shared with the top echelons of the Indian Government."

In Sahota's judgment two things are important for India. One is democracy, the other is secularism. Sahota believes that for India to really grow, the classes must take a back seat, and the masses must become the center of focused attention. That would mean more wealth creation overall, and the economy getting bigger. Also social inequalities would come down. A scenario difficult to script, but not quite impossible, says the cardiologist.

He told the RSS leaders that even though Sikhs have contributed very significantly to Indian history, and defended the nation from invaders for centuries, their role is not sufficiently illustrated in Indian history books. Sahota also pointed out that with perhaps the exception of Punjab, the rest of India does not know who Guru Tegh Bahadur Ji was and why he gave his life in 1675 at a place near the Red Fort, Delhi—which now has the historical and famous Gurdwara Sis Ganj Sahib, *Sis* meaning head.

Solution:

He told the RSS brass that including topics about the Sikh religion and the role of Sikhs in defending India from invasions for centuries is not Sikh history but a part of Indian history. But for the sacrifices of the Sikhs and Sikh Gurus, India would not be a democracy, nor would it be a secular nation today. Sahota says that both Vaidya and Bhaigaih had readily agreed with him. They also informed him that the deficiency in the school curriculum was being

LEFT: Dr Tony Grover, a successful Orthopedic Surgeon based in Las Vegas (right) with his wife Monica next to him, and the Sahotas. **RIGHT:** Tony with daughter Avalon

taken care of, and that necessary steps had been initiated in that direction by the Indian Government.

GLOBAL VIOLENCE AND CONFLICTS

Sahota's opinions and judgments in this area are based on extensive research and knowledge over the years. He believes that it is critical in every situation of conflict and violence to identify the cause at the earliest by going straight to the root of the problem, and systematically treating it. "It is no good treating the symptom. We need to identify the cause. Otherwise all conflicts will linger," he says, citing a few prime examples.

According to the heart doctor, there are two main problems related to violence and terror in the world today. All other similar problems are inevitably related to these two problems, either directly, or indirectly. They are:

● Tensions between India and Pakistan over Kashmir.
● Tensions between Israel and Palestine.

India and Pakistan

Sahota was a young boy of just six when the horrors of partition unfolded in India. The annihilation of hundreds of thousands of innocents on either side (India and Pakistan) by frenzied mobs in one of the bloodiest holocausts became one of the lowest points in the history of world violence. The maximum damage was inflicted in the province of undivided British Punjab. Sahota's family lived in Garhdiwala, a town that after August 15, 1947 would become part of Indian Punjab, close to the border with newly-formed West Pakistan. In fact, Garhdiwala is 80 miles east of the Indo-Pakistan border town of Attari. As a young man he experienced what partition could inflict. Thousands, on either side, were forced to leave their fields, homes, businesses, and run away to safety, their dreams totally shattered. They were pushed into a dark future that refugees usually stare at. Penury and fear accompanied them to the other side of the borders, and survival in many cases became a pointless daily grind. In most cases the refugees themselves had narrowly escaped after having witnessed loved ones losing their lives to mindless violence. In the new camps where they sought shelter, the refugees were left to the mercy of heartless Government functionaries.

Congressman Ed Royce who's known Harvinder Sahota for a very long time mentioned at a recent function in California that the doctor's prescription for reducing tension between the two Sub-Continental neighbors is a good one. Royce found Sahota's thinking quite neutral and his opinions pretty much fair to all sides. Royce said that the cardiologist firmly believes that instead of spending billions of dollars on armaments and defense which both India and Pakistan have been doing since 1947, the money should instead be spent prudently on the welfare of the people of both nations with an express objective of alleviating poverty. If required, the US can play a balancing role in sitting down both sides on the same table and helping resolve long-standing disputes. "The only thing that violence begets," says Sahota, "is more violence." It is a fact that is quite hard to digest, but is a timeless truth nonetheless.

Israel and Palestine

Sahota elaborates on his views, and admits that he is on the same page on the Israel-Palestine subject as Ambassador Dennis Ross with whom he interacted at a program in May 2017. Ross was involved in the Israeli-Palestinian peace process during the Bush and Clinton administrations. Listed below are solutions provided by Sahota:

- A deeper and finer understanding of both Eastern and Western cultures. Both cultures react differently to threats, intimidations, death and destruction.
- Determined efforts on the part of political leaders on both sides to put the lives and welfare of their people, especially those in the disputed zone, ahead of their own political futures.
- Mediation efforts by neutral third parties, including involving the United Nations.
- In order to build confidence on either side, the US Ambassador to Israel should be a Muslim, and the one to Palestine should be a Jew. The US representatives handling this issue should be a Muslim and a Jew. This would serve as a confidence building measure.

Sahota says that Ambassador Ross said that there was no problem with this kind of arrangement. "Solve the Kashmir and Palestine problems satisfactorily and 90 per cent of the globe's terrorism will disappear overnight. All the fragmented terror groups that keep mushrooming from time to time will stop taking innocent lives," Sahota says.

Your terrorist is my freedom fighter

Sahota says this is an age-old issue. Those who are fighting against the Indian Army in Kashmir call themselves freedom fighters. The Indian Government, of course, dubs them terrorists. Likewise, George Washington was declared a terrorist by the British, but he remains an American hero who continues to be on every US currency note, and was also the nation's first President. "If the British had got hold of him, in all probability it would have culminated in a swift trial and his hanging," says Sahota, reflecting on how viewpoints differ. Likewise, Indians who were struggling to free the nation from foreign rule were often times labeled terrorists by the British. There are several cases of *Gadarites* who were caught, tried, hanged or sentenced to life imprisonment in the cellular jail in Andaman and Nicobar Islands for trying to free India. "For the British, the *Gadarites* were terrorists. For Indians, they were freedom fighters," the cardiologist points out.

"Why the Nobel Prize could never be conferred on

The Sahotas with John E Forsyte, President, Pacific Symphony (right) who arranged for the performance of *The Passions of Ramakrishna* at Costa Mesa, California and Carnegie Hall, New York, and Dr Jo Ellen Chatham, Director, The Center for Public Policy, Concordia University Irvine. Dr Chatham has said in an interview that she was very impressed by Sahota's intellectual curiosity and his knowledge about so many subjects beyond medicine

Mahatma Gandhi whose life epitomized non-violence and *Ahimsa*? Did the committee not find him a man of peace?" asks Sahota. Likewise, he points out, that Nelson Mandela too was a terrorist in the eyes of the rulers of South Africa who kept him imprisoned in Robben Island for 29 years for wanting to free his land from the clutches of the oppressive, apartheid-practicing regime. Similarly, Menachem Begin who was the leader of Irgun before the creation of Israel, was seen as a terrorist threat by the British. Later, after becoming Israel's sixth Prime Minister, he signed a peace treaty with Egypt in 1979, for which he shared the Noble Prize for Peace with Anwar Sadat. "Once a terrorist, Begin became a messenger of peace. The lesson is that we should be very careful before

calling someone a terrorist," says Sahota.

A TET-A-TET WITH DENNIS ROSS

In May 2017, Sahota spent a considerably long time talking to Ambassador Dennis Ross at a program in Orange County. Ross had been heavily involved in the Israeli-Palestinian peace process during the Bush and Clinton administrations. He assisted the Israelis and Palestinians to reach the 1995 Interim Agreement, and also successfully brokered the 1997 Hebron Accord. He also facilitated the 1994 Israel-Jordan peace treaty, and worked hard to bring Israel and Syria together. He was awarded the Presidential Medal for Distinguished Federal Civilian Service by President Clinton, while Secretaries Baker and

LEFT: Standing (L-R) Dr Sridharan, Dr Sahota, Dr Gandhi at the North Wales Hospital. Among those seated are Superintendent Dr Biagi (center) and Dr Bapat (second from right). Incidentally, it is the British 'hybrid' health care system that Sahota admires the most. **RIGHT:** Dr Sahota (standing fifth from left) seen alongside professors, staff, residents and interns at the Regina General Hospital in Canada in 1977. He was Chief Resident in Medicine. Seated in the center is Dr Gerald Ewing, Director of Programmes, at Regina. It was Dr Ewing who had helped arrange for a fellowship for Sahota in Los Angeles when the cardiologist decided that he would move on from Regina. Sahota, in fact, had turned down a lucrative offer to stay on with the hospital in Rochester, New York, in order to meet a commitment he had made to Regina General while still in the U.K. Interestingly, he'd have earned more than ten times had he stayed back in Rochester and not gone to Regina

Albright presented him with the State Department's highest award. Ross told Sahota that during negotiations, he had suggested that Israel should go in for block development along the 1967 border—a demarcation line set out in the 1949 Armistice Agreements between Israel and its neighbors Egypt, Jordan, Lebanon and Syria. This would take away only 1.7 percent of the West Bank. Israel should give an equal amount of land to Palestine somewhere else. And with the help of modern technology Israel could resolve the water problems in the West Bank.

Among several conflict situations in the world, Sahota has been following the one in Israel and Palestine very closely. Sometime during the period when Benjamin Netanyahu was in his first term in office as Prime Minister of Israel

(June 1996-July 1999), Sahota had written to him, and also to King Hussein of Jordan—whose rule extended through four decades of Arab-Israeli conflict—and Egyptian President Muhammad Hosni El Sayed Mubarak, saying that the idea of a buffer zone with a neutral army that had been mooted was a good one. When heated discussions were on between Israel and Palestine, a neutral army had been proposed. Both the UN Peacekeeping Force and the US Army were considered as viable options for being stationed in these places. But both Israel and Palestine rejected the proposal.

Sahota came up with a third option. He suggested that one of the most neutral armies that could be stationed in the conflict area could be drawn from retired officers and other ranks of the Sikh Regiment in India. They would not